WHOLESOME

COMMUNICATION

a guide to a spiritual conversation

J.A. KNEPPER

Translated by **Theodore Plantinga**

Pastoral Perspectives I

INHERITANCE PUBLICATIONS
NEERLANDIA, ALBERTA, CANADA

Canadian Cataloguing in Publication Data

Knepper, J.A.
  Wholesome Communication

  (Pastoral perspectives ; 1)
  Translation of: Het heilzame gesprek.
  ISBN 0-921100-13-2

  1. Communication - Religious aspects - Christianity.
  2. Conversation - Religious aspects - Christianity.
  3. Pastoral counseling. I. Title. II. Series.
  BV4319.K6313 1989   253.5   C89-091484-2

Translated by Theodore Plantinga

Original published as *Het Heilzame Gesprek*,(1988)
by Oosterbaan & Le Cointre, Goes, the Netherlands.
Published with permission.

ISBN 0-921100-13-2

Printed in Canada by
Premier Printing Ltd. Winnipeg, MB

TABLE OF CONTENTS

Chapter 1

Holy Conversations

> *And as for you, the anointing which you received*
> *from Him abides in you, and you have no need*
> *for any one to teach you; but as His anointing*
> *teaches you about all things, and is true and is*
> *not a lie, and just as it has taught you, you abide*
> *in Him.*   I John 2:27

Since this book forms part of a series called "Pastoral Perspectives," the obvious title that comes to mind for it is "Pastoral Conversations," or perhaps "Pastoral Communication."
There are various reasons why I did not choose such a title.
The most important of those reasons lies in the text quoted
above. This text makes it clear — as do other passages in the
Bible — that talking about salvation in Christ is not reserved
for the "pastor" or some other office-bearer, such as an elder.
It is true that the pastors and elders, as shepherds of the congregation (pastor means shepherd), are ministers of Christ's
salvation, and that one way they carry out their task of min-
istry is in pastoral conversations. Yet to recognize this is not to
deny that "ordinary" members of the congregation should not
or could not conduct such conversations as well. An essential
characteristic of spiritual care in the New Testament is that
it is carried out by the members of the congregation as they
care for one another. Every member of the congregation has a
responsibility for the other members of the body, a responsibility to share with them the joy and comfort we have in Christ,
a responsibility to encourage, comfort and admonish them, a
responsibility, in short, to help and to serve.

The apostle Peter is very clear about this matter when he says: "As each one has received a special gift, employ it in serving one another, as good stewards of the manifold grace of God. Whoever speaks, let him speak, as it were, the utterances of God; whoever serves, let him do so as by the strength which God supplies; so that in all things God may be glorified through Jesus Christ, to whom belongs the glory and dominion forever and ever" (I Pet. 4:10–11).

The kind of conversation and communication I am writing about can be called "holy," or perhaps "wholesome." In everyday language, the things we call wholesome are rich in blessing: they tend toward our benefit. This ordinary meaning is also applicable when it comes to conversation that focuses on salvation in Christ. It is interesting to note that *heil,* which is the Dutch word for salvation, is related to the Dutch word for *whole.* Salvation, it seems, has to do with making us whole.

Let's think for a moment about the content of a wholesome or holy conversation with a person who is sick, or is suffering from the frailties of aging, or is in danger of starving, or is handicapped or depressed, or is lonely or apathetic or is subject to temptations, or is in mourning, or is laboring under severe financial difficulties, perhaps caused by unemployment. We could be talking about a conversation with someone having marriage difficulties, or facing problems in raising children, or suffering from sexual maladjustment. In such conversations we are dealing with people who are torn by conflict, or have wandered away, or are in the process of wandering away. Let's also consider conversations with those who have reason to rejoice, whether because of marriage or the birth of a child or an appointment just received or a degree that has been awarded. Or perhaps the reason for celebration is public profession of faith, or triumph over one's doubts, or a stirring testimony in one's old age about God's great works. Or the person you are talking with might be rejoicing in children and grandchildren. Holy conversation can concern itself with God's work in gathering His church, or with the administration of the Word and sacraments, or with commandments and prayer, or with false teachings, or with all sorts of everyday questions about how to live as a Christian. The subject of such a conversation could be the battle we fight against sin and the future we and our children face. It is always a type of conversation that does not focus on the externals of life but penetrates to the center of our personal existence, thus touching not only on our rationality but also on our emotions, our motives, our soul, our body, all our powers, and on our heart as the very center of our existence.

Chapter 2

Communication

Anyone who is not used to conversing will not have much success conducting spiritual conversations. The ability to converse is a creational gift. Therefore we should first review what speaking and listening involve by nature; then we should go on to explore the respect in which these beautiful gifts were spoiled by the fall into sin, with the result that our efforts at communication became inadequate. When God created man in His image and likeness to be His representative on earth, He equipped Adam and Eve with excellent gifts. The God who spoke also taught them to speak so that they would be able to understand His words and respond to Him in their songs and prayers. Moreover, human beings could use the gift of speech to communicate with one another.

Although we are already speaking of "communication" and "means of communication," we will see later (in Chapter 5) what actually goes on when human beings communicate, and what difficulties can get in the way. Communication is such a complicated process that we keep discovering new facets of it. There are countless books that take up this subject, and they all seem to disagree with one another. Thus one could choose any one of a hundred or more definitions!

In this context I will deal with only two definitions. The first one is this: communication is the sharing or exchanging of (information with regard to) a message with the intention of coming to a common understanding of that message. We find a number of elements within this definition. *Sharing* by itself is *one-sided* communication. It may result in an understanding of what has been shared, but in many cases we cannot be sure whether the proper understanding has been attained. But if there is an *exchange* of information, we can speak of *two-sided* communication, in which case we have some indication whether the message got across. It is also possible that more information about the message is requested so that the message can be *tested.* Or the person sending the message can receive "feedback," whether verbally or by means of a non-verbal gesture, such as a small nod. For example, a person might say, "John, I'm going to bring this letter to the mailbox." The person being addressed nods to show that he has understood the message. Here we have a non-verbal indication that there is a common understanding of the message.

A second definition of communication to be considered is this: communication is a process that takes place between people in a certain way (whether verbally or non-verbally); it is an event in a certain spatio-temporal situation and usually has a specific goal, such as the passing on of information, that is, information with a news value, information that is not always understood or interpreted properly. In this definition the emphasis falls much more on the situation: *which* persons, *which* means, *which* circumstances. All of these are determinative for the success or failure of the attempt at communication.

Just how important the circumstances are when it comes to communication is something we all know from experience. For example, we sense that we cannot reprove someone if there are other people present who have nothing to do with the matter at hand. To conduct a confidential conversation, we prefer a quiet environment.

What is of particular importance is the relationship between the participants in the conversation. We are generally inclined to pay attention only to the *content* of what is said; yet speakers also send out certain non-verbal signals about how their words are to be received, whether seriously or only as a joke, whether as information that must be taken to heart or as "take it or leave it" advice. Normally a person does not say,

"This is a request," or, "This is a command," but on the relational level it is clear to the hearer in what spirit the content of the message is supposed to be received.

There are many different possibilities when it comes to relationships between people engaging in a conversation. One person may take the leading role in the conversation, relegating the other to the role of following. In a conversation about spiritual matters between a minister and a member of his congregation, the minister will normally take the lead. But if the topic changes to something about which the church member is quite knowledgeable, the leadership in the conversation will probably change hands: then the minister may well be dependent on the information which his conversation partner injects into the discussion.

But there are other patterns possible for a conversation, such as equality, which means that neither partner leads and neither follows. The remarkable thing here is that the conflicts in the conversation do not have much to do with the *content* of what is said; rather, they arise largely from the definition of the situation! Take the case of a conversation between a father and his seventeen-year-old son: normally you would expect that the father would take the leading role. But suppose the son thinks he is now old (and wise) enough to talk with his father as an equal. In that case his father is not supposed to say to him, "I want you to do this or that"; instead he will have to produce reasons and answer the arguments his son comes up with — that's the proper way to come to agreement, thinks the son. But if such a son (or a daughter, for that matter) is relegated to the follower's role in the conversation, the thought will soon come up: "I can't talk with Mom or Dad — they just refuse to listen."

It goes without saying that if both parties to a conversation want to take either the leader's role or the follower's role, there will be conflict. If I take the leading role and my partner accepts this state of affairs, I am confirmed in my conduct, and my conversation partner is in turn confirmed in his role.

But suppose he says to himself, "Who does he think he is? He seems to imagine he can call the shots here!" And suppose he goes on to ask me, as the people of Israel asked Moses: "Who made you judge over us?" At that point I am being directly challenged. One way of reacting in such a situation is simply to pretend you didn't hear what was said. That way you may succeed in shaking the confidence of your conversation partner, who may then begin to doubt himself. At that point he will have to make a choice — whether to continue with this battle and try to win recognition from you, or to accept the situation in which you are placing him. In some cases this would mean withdrawing from the situation, like Moses running away from Egypt to Midian.

In summary we can say that communication is a process we are rarely able to analyze precisely. We can exchange thoughts and feelings with one another. We have words and gestures at our command. We operate on two levels at once: the content level (what we say) and the relational level. We may understand one another completely, or partially, or not at all. Sometimes the feelings that animate our conversation partner don't get through to us, and on other occasions we do pick them up but don't quite know what to do with them. Good communication takes an enormous amount of practice!

Chapter 3

First Intermezzo:
Jesus and Nicodemus

> *Now there was a man of the Pharisees, named Nicodemus, a ruler of the Jews; this man came to Him by night, and said to Him, "Rabbi, we know that You have come from God as a teacher; for no one can do these signs that You do unless God is with him."*
>
> John 3:1–2

In drawing on certain passages from the Bible to illustrate the points I wish to make, I am well aware that the Bible is not supposed to be used as a handbook of technical information about communication. Not even the conversations *Jesus* conducted should be given an exemplary status, so that we would say of them, "Let's observe very carefully how the Lord carried on a conversation, for who could have been more perfect in speaking with others than He?"

The first reason why we are *not* to imitate the conversations of Jesus is that He was without sin. He knew just what was in a person. We can do no more than *guess* what lives within another person, and often we make mistakes. As a perfect human being, Jesus could sense infallibly when a person came to him with evil intentions, or when someone was pretending. As the Son of God He not only knew the Scriptures perfectly but was Himself the living Word. Since none of these perfections apply to us, we cannot conduct conversations in the very same manner as our Savior.

There is another reason to bear in mind. It is my view that the conversations conducted by Jesus are not reproduced for us in the Bible *literally* but in summary fashion and thus might include only the major points. You can check up on this for yourself by reading aloud his conversations with Nicodemus, with the Samaritan woman, and with the two men on their way to Emmaus. Even if you read slowly and deliberately, it should not take you more than about five or six minutes to go through any one of them. Now, no one really believes that the actual conversations were as brief as that. They must have taken at least half an hour, and in the case of the men walking to Emmaus, two hours is a more likely estimate. What the Bible gives us out of these conversations is the message for the church of all ages; it does not give us a word-by-word transcript that would enable us to follow the course of the conversation sentence by sentence.

There is one more consideration to take into account. The purpose of Jesus' conversations was not the same as the purpose you or I might have in conducting a spiritual conversation. Jesus spoke to people to convince them that *He* was the Messiah, the one who had been sent by the Father. That was also why He performed miracles — to support that message. Those who heard Him talking would then say to themselves, "Surely such great wonders couldn't be performed by anyone other than the great Rabbi! Is he then the Messiah?" The man who was born blind said, "He is a prophet. If he had not been sent by God, he would not have been able to do anything." But because of the personal conversation Jesus conducted with him, he was eventually able to confess, "I believe, Lord: I believe You are the Son of God."

We will now listen to the conversation between Jesus and Nicodemus. As we explore this conversation carefully, we will see illustrations of some of the matters discussed in this little book.

Nicodemus was an important person, a ruler of the Jews

and a member of the group known as the Pharisees. He was
also a righteous man. When the other Pharisees heard about
the words Jesus spoke and the miracles He performed, the main
thought that arose in their minds was that His influence would
cost them some of their power. This had to be avoided at all
costs; His influence would have to be kept to a minimum. If
efforts to block His influence should fail, they would simply
have to get rid of Him.

But that was not how Nicodemus thought. He paid attention to the content of Jesus' words and to the wonders He
performed as signs. When he thought it over, he came to the
conclusion that this man had come from God as a teacher. And
so he decided he would like to talk with Him, but this desire
represented something of a problem, for he did not want his
colleagues among the Pharisees to think ill of him or reproach
him. Therefore he decided he would seek Jesus out during
the night. We do not know whether this night-time visit was
arranged in advance. The fact is simply that the Lord Jesus
received him.

Perhaps this is the first matter that should draw our attention: *Jesus imposed no conditions.* You or I might have
been inclined to say, "If this man is ashamed to come in the
daytime, then he should not come at all, for I do not believe in
secret meetings." Or perhaps, "I'm quite willing to make time
for him, but I will not sacrifice my night's rest — that's going
too far!" Or perhaps, "I just won't talk with any member of
that hypocritical group, the Pharisees." But the Lord did not
say anything of this sort. Instead He made Himself available
for a conversation.

In an encounter, as in any genuine instance of communication, it must first be established whether the two parties
are equals, as opposed to one being greater or more important
than the other. Nicodemus immediately made it clear how he
thought about this: he called Jesus "Rabbi," thus recognizing Him as a teacher sent by God. And since he himself was
also a rabbi, he was proposing to talk with Jesus on the basis

of equality. Given the conception of things he brought to the conversation, he surely was not doing Jesus an injustice, as far as he was concerned; rather, he was honoring Him. After all, Nicodemus was a ruler of the Jews, a man of considerable importance! His great mistake was that although he did look upon Jesus as a teacher sent by God, he did not acknowledge Him as *the* Teacher, the Messiah who was to come and had now finally arrived. Thus there should really have been no thought in his mind of speaking with Jesus on the basis of equality!

When we pay attention to the *content* of the conversation, it *might* appear that Jesus simply began with the Kingdom of God and the necessity of being born again. But this is not the way it happened. Nicodemus had said that the wonders Jesus performed were signs that God was indeed with Him. But what did those signs really indicate? When John the Baptist asked whether Jesus was indeed the Messiah and raised the question whether he should be awaiting someone else, the Lord Himself pointed to those wonders as indications that the prophecies of Isaiah were being fulfilled, which meant that the day of salvation was dawning. The one who is anointed with the Spirit of the LORD brings a joyful message to the meek, and through the power of the Spirit He performs all the miracles about which the prophets had prophesied. And so Nicodemus should really have concluded not just that a rabbi sent from God had come but that the Kingdom of God and *the* Rabbi had come.

The Pharisees looked ahead to that Kingdom without any fear or foreboding, for they believed that when it dawned, they could present themselves as righteous. They thought they had earned this designation by keeping the law. But now Jesus came along, saying that the Kingdom of God was only open to a person if he was born anew, which meant that he (Nicodemus) could not enter it. This was an intolerable thought for Nicodemus, and so he rejected it. He did not ask why this new birth should be necessary; he simply argued that it is impossible. A man cannot very well enter his mother's womb again! Surely Jesus did not mean to demand something impossible!

Jesus answered him, "Unless a man is born of water and the Spirit, he cannot enter the Kingdom of God." In other words, what Jesus was demanding was indeed possible, but not for the person who lives according to the flesh — not even through God's Spirit.

Through the expression on his face (a non-verbal signal), Nicodemus let Jesus know that this statement amazed and perplexed him. The Lord responded to this signal when He said, "Do not be amazed at the need of this new birth. The Spirit can be compared to the wind. The wind is not something you can take hold of; you can't direct it or force it to go this way or that. The wind is free and mighty; you don't know where it comes from or where it will come to rest." But even if a person does not know and understand these things, it does not occur to him to say, "The wind doesn't exist." After all, we do hear the sound of the wind. And that's also how it is with the Spirit, explained Jesus, and with everyone who is born of the Spirit. The Spirit certainly exists and acts, even if human beings cannot understand how.

By this point Nicodemus was not so sure of himself any more. Instead of claiming that the new birth was impossible, he asked how it comes about. Jesus then made him even more uncertain, for He said, "Are you a teacher of Israel and do not understand these things?" (Here we have a reproach, a value judgment.) "Such an important teacher of the people of Israel, who knows the law and the prophets, should surely have some knowledge of this important matter! Anyone who reads the Scriptures carefully will observe that they testify of Me."

Nicodemus did not ask anything more: he listened to the instruction which the Lord now gave him about heavenly things, about God's Counsel of Peace, about the only-begotten Son who was sent into the world to save the world through faith in Him. This Son will be lifted up, just as Moses lifted up the serpent in the wilderness. Through His suffering He will save the world.

We do not know how Nicodemus responded to this teaching. Did he accept it or reject it? It is quite well possible that the conversation was concluded with a comment by Nicodemus: "I must think all these things over and search the Scriptures some more." But *one* thing surely became clear to him: with his righteousness he would not be able to enter the Kingdom of God. He could enter the Kingdom only through faith in this Rabbi, the Son of God, a faith created in him by the Spirit.

Chapter 4

Non-Verbal Communication

Voice and silence

Speaking doesn't only involve the use of our vocal cords and mouth and lips and tongue — it draws on the person as a totality. When we look at all the non-verbal functions one by one, we begin with the voice. We are then focusing not on the words but on the sound of the voice — on whether it is loud or soft, on whether the tone is pitched high or low, on the regularity in the speech rhythm, on the structure and completeness of the sentences, on the pauses that are made or not made as the speaker rushes to his conclusion. For example, if you have a message that is very sad for its hearer, you will choose your words very carefully, but at the same time (probably without even thinking about it) you will find yourself talking slowly, with various pauses. And if the person you are addressing is someone dear to you, you will speak in a low tone of voice in order to express your sympathy in non-verbal fashion as well. Perhaps you need these non-verbal elements especially because you find words inadequate.

What do the eyes say?

Everyone knows from his own experience that eye contact (or the lack of it) can have quite an influence on a conversation. Perhaps we sense this most strongly when we try to talk to someone only to have him turn his back to us. In such a situation, a conversation is hardly possible at all. But if you look your conversation partner in the eye, you can see something of the inwardness of the speaking and listening man or woman with whom you are talking. Sometimes you will read interest in a person's eyes, but you can also find boundless boredom or sheer lack of interest expressed in the way he looks at you. It is significant that we use our eyes to signal that we are nearly finished with something we are saying; this lets the other person know he should be ready to jump in and say something in response. Particularly difficult is a situation in which someone's gaze is continually fixed on the face of his partner, or the opposite of such a situation, when one of the partners to the conversation looks constantly at the floor or at the ceiling or out the window.

Facial expression and mimicry

Laughter and smiles are indications of pleasure. We can use not just our eyes but also the muscles of our face and our mouth to make our conversation partner aware that we are happy. Happiness is an emotion that can be read on a person's face. The same could be said of amazement, disappointment, anxiety, anger, and contempt. Sympathy and antipathy are feelings toward others that can also be brought to expression through mimicry; that is to say, we can *act* as though we are sympathetic or hostile. Sometimes, out of politeness, we put on a friendly face in order to mask what we are really feeling toward our discussion partner.

In a conversation we react constantly to both the words and the facial expressiveness of the person we are talking with. If we do not understand something we can come right out and say so, but it is quicker not to interrupt and instead let a question mark be registered on our face. The person who is speaking then sees that he must react, and so he clarifies what he is saying. But if he reads agreement on our face, we confirm him in what he is saying, which means, as a rule, that he is encouraged to talk further along the same line.

Postures and movements

When we focus on the non-verbal language of the entire body, we must distinguish between *postures* (such as sitting or standing) and *movements* (such as the gestures we make). This division, however, does not account fully for such phenomena as nervous conduct, hurried breathing, trembling, shaking, sweating, tense muscles, and so forth. We should realize that our conversation partner often spots such things even before we ourselves are aware of them. And the conversation is influenced by them in a way that simply cannot be reversed or undone. If you are uneasy and tense in your conduct, you will make your conversation partner nervous. When we take up the proper posture for conversation (Chapter 6), the first principle we will hit upon is that we should be physically relaxed.

But that's not the only thing to be mentioned. We also need the "right" posture for the situation. If you are talking with someone who is sitting down, you should be seated as well. It is much more effective to sit down by a sickbed than to remain standing. If you are rebuking someone or dismissing him from his job, you will have to assume a different posture than if you are trying to comfort a person. In the latter case I can well imagine that you would take the person you are talking with by the hand, but not in the former case.

Taking someone by the hand counts as a gesture: it is one of a number of possible gestures whereby we make physical contact with another person. We can hold a person's hand for a longer or shorter time, give him a tap on the shoulder, kiss him, embrace him, or caress him. Sometimes a gesture of this sort is the last means available to us in the effort to communicate. Think of people who are very seriously ill, or of aged people who have lost their minds. We can no longer reach them with words, but they will be less a little lonely and anxious if we hold their hand or caress them. In general it can be said that gestures serve to reinforce our words: think of the effect of a handshake when an agreement is made. I saw this point nicely illustrated once when I participated in a communion service at a Reformed church in Paris: after the celebration many of the communicants shook hands or exchanged a kiss.

Our gestures may also betray us: they can show our conversation partner that our words are not genuine. If you say, "We'll just have to take the time to discuss this matter calmly and thoroughly," and then begin looking at your watch repeatedly once it does appear to be taking some time, your conversation partner will know you were not sincere.

The spatial dimension

In general it can be said that the closer people sit to one another, the more they have to do with each other. If you are within forty centimeters (about thirteen inches) of another person, you are within his "intimate space." You should only be that close if you are indeed "intimate" with that person; thus a minister or elder or deacon or a member of the congregation coming by for a visit should *not* be that close! The space within which a holy conversation takes place could perhaps be called "informal personal space." A distance of about 120 centimeters (roughly forty inches) would be ideal for such a conversation.

The placement of the chairs is also important. If it can be avoided, they should not be directly opposite one another, for that makes the conversation seem like an interview. It is better to have the chairs at right angles to each other. If you are receiving someone for the purpose of conversation, you should ask yourself whether your conversation partner will enjoy being in your study (perhaps it is full to overflowing with books) or in your office (where everything may point to efficiency) or in your living room (where you may have to move some things off a chair to make it possible for him to sit down). In short, *you* may be completely at home in the place where you receive him, but your guest may be a bit frightened or intimidated by it. Likewise, if you are visiting someone who is sick, whether in the hospital or in his own home, bear in mind (assuming that he is allowed to get out of bed) that he would rather talk with you while sitting in a chair than when he is flat on his back.

The whole person

In a conversation you are present with your whole person. Even before a word is spoken, quite a bit of information has been exchanged. The clothes you are wearing indicate whether you are at work or on your free time or dressed up for some special occasion. And as for your voice, let's hope that it's pleasant to listen to, but it may be hoarse one day, or somewhat squeaky. You may also find yourself stuttering.

And think about your face, which may be happy or reflect disappointment. Your conversation partner may read in your face that you are calm — or perhaps that you are anxious. Consider also the way you wear your hair. If you are a man, you may have a beard or a mustache or sideburns. And if you are a woman, your hair may be curled, or styled in accord with the latest fashion with the help of a hairdresser.

How much care your conversation partner has taken with his appearance (or how little) says a great deal about him. And you will notice whether there is some scent emanating from him, which may tell you something about his job. Does he use a deodorant? Does he have sweaty feet or clammy hands? Does he cover his body odors with a perfume or scent? What sorts of products does he use for personal hygiene? Whatever scent or lack of odor you detect will have some bearing on your conversation with him.

Let me now give you two examples to indicate how important non-verbal communication can be when it comes to holy conversations. An evangelist who goes from door to door as he talks with people about the gospel puts himself in situations in which virtually everything on the non-verbal side of communication runs contrary to his hopes. It is hard to get a conversation going at the door, and he will not easily make it clear what his purpose is in relation is to the person he meets there. (He may well be taken for a salesman.) Because he is unknown, he will not quickly be appreciated and trusted either. After all, who would want to carry on a significant conversation with the front door standing half open? And if you allow a stranger to enter your house, don't you run a certain risk, even if he does claim to be an evangelist? There are not many people who will make time for someone without an appointment — especially someone who seems to want to discuss some ill-defined matter. And so, anyone who goes door-to-door to evangelize does not have a great deal of hope of getting a response when he rings a given doorbell.

My second example is a missionary who deals with natives having no knowledge of Western culture. Such a missionary comes with enormous non-verbal power in terms of the things he possesses, such as his clothes, his watch, his house with a refrigerator (which may serve to keep beer chilled), his books and radio, perhaps a motorboat or even an airplane, his money, the medicines he has access to, and probably many other things of which we are not even aware. The people on the mission field with whom he talks about the gospel will weigh all these possessions against what their gods have managed to give them, and they may soon conclude that the white god is superior. They would be better off believing in the white man's god!

Chapter 5

Communication Problems

All men are liars.
Ps. 116:11

When communication is successful, it is a beautiful experience. It is wonderful to share in the thoughts and feelings of another person and thereby experience communion with him.

Unfortunately, what we find all too often is that communication is broken or corrupt. Sinful man remains trapped in deceit and constantly wants to deal with people on the basis of lies. When the Bible uses the word "liar," what it means first of all is someone who is unreliable. Note that this is the very opposite of the assurance regarding God that what *He* says is fixed and true and sure. God's Word is truth (John 17:17); people can build on it, for it stands firm. We can say our amen to it. But when *people* speak, what comes forth from them all too often is deceit, falsehood, idleness, flattery, glib language, faithlessness, and even betrayal. You simply can't build on what people tell you.

We will now see how communication is manipulated — whether consciously or unconsciously — when love and faithfulness are missing.

No openness — when there is no trust

There are not all that many people whose heart comes to open expression through what they say. We are not so quick to reveal what lies deep within us. When we are in conversation with the LORD, we are not able to hide anything, of course. This is what Psalm 139 teaches us: "Thou dost understand my thoughts from afar and art intimately acquainted with all my ways. Where can I go from Thy Spirit? Even the darkness is not dark to Thee" (vs. 2, 3, 7, 12). In our conversation with God, in our prayer, we do not need to hide anything, for the LORD is loving and faithful. Whatever we say to our Father is safe with Him.

But that's not the way it works with *people*. If we have the courage to speak about things that concern us at the deepest level, we are sometimes shaken and disappointed when we see how others handle what we have entrusted to them. How loveless and faithless people can be! Once you have had this kind of experience, you will guard your concerns and doubts and problems instead of talking about them freely. Yet talking about them could bring you so much spiritual health and wholesomeness.

The absence of "openness" is not hard to understand. But there is still this question to be asked: How can we encourage people to be truly open?

The answer should be evident from what I said above. If trust is not present, we will first have to win it — or perhaps win it back. Obviously, the way to do this is to be reliable, which means dealing sensitively and confidentially with what people entrust to us about their personal lives. Officebearers and other functionaries who gain knowledge of confidential matters in the course of their work are sometimes to be preferred when talking about extremely personal matters.

Furthermore, we should all bear in mind that trust has to be *won*! This is not the sort of thing in which you are likely to succeed the very first time out; rather, on the first visit with someone you will probably stick to superficial matters. You may do a fair amount of talking, and in the process you may get some sense of what can be talked about. After such a beginning the time may come when the person you have talked with says, "There is something I would like to talk with you about. Do you suppose you can make some time?" When this point in the conversation is reached, you may find that you ask yourself, "Why is it so necessary that we talk about this *now?*" Yet what unfolds in such a case is not all that hard to understand. The really important things come out in a conversation once you have demonstrated not just that you are willing to listen carefully but also that you have been listening attentively to *all* that was said earlier in the relationship.

Finally, we should bear in mind that many men and women have great difficulty expressing in words that which concerns them deeply. They fear that powerful emotions may break loose when they begin to talk — and they would really prefer to keep those emotions in check.

Manipulation of information through egoism

I will not comment on the fact that when we lie or slander someone, we are (among other things) giving out incorrect information. The point I want to focus on instead is that when we speak, what we say is often "colored" by objectives we have set for ourselves. This could mean, for example, that we are not really interested in what the other person has to say but wish only to get our own story out. Anxiety that we may be feeling also has a great influence on what we say and hear. If we are afraid of our conversation partner, we may remain silent about all sorts of things. We may also be afraid of what might be said to us, and so we try to keep our partner from speaking, perhaps by talking a blue streak ourselves. *Curiosity* may lead us to pose ever more penetrating questions — not because the answers represent matters we should know about (after all, we are not psychiatrists!) but because we have an unhealthy interest in getting the other person to talk. We are proud when we get our conversation partner to tell us things about himself that he later wishes he had not said.

Questions rooted in curiosity are not the only ones that are out of bounds; *suggestive* questions are also contraband. When we ask such questions, our conversation partner does not have the opportunity to consider the matter peacefully and then formulate an answer — instead the answer has already been prepared for him. Sometimes we put on pressure to agree by injecting our personal weight into his deliberations and saying, "Surely you would agree with me that ...."

We should also pause for a moment to consider the role of *presuppositions* as they are sometimes built into questions: "We can take it, surely, that you would rather not return to your house." When we ask suggestive questions or pose questions grounded in curiosity or presuppose things, we are not manifesting much respect for the person we are talking with. Is he such a dependent creature that we have to prompt him in his answers? Is there really any need for us to try and steer the conversation?

If you are hungry for respect and regard yourself as a very important person, you will probably wind up talking a lot about yourself and making much of your own accomplishments. You are then busy stroking yourself and hoping to win applause from the other person, who is not your conversation partner but your *target*. At that point it can no longer be said that you are talking *with* someone.

Lack of understanding, lack of sympathy

To understand or grasp something involves taking hold of it. When we hear words and sentences uttered by someone, we try to take hold of them in order to make them our own. There is something foolish about this process: what we wind up taking hold of is generally not what the speaker has in mind. The reason for this is that each of us brings his personal history to the effort to understand. The content of the apparatus through which we filter and process a speaker's words is dependent on the experiences we have had, our formal education, our vocation in life, our age, our ideas, our memories — and all of these are individual factors that vary from person to person.

Consider the term "concentration camp" as an example. Small children don't know what it means. Somewhat older children may ask, "Doesn't it have something to do with the second world war?" Adults may say, "Yes, it must have been horrible." But someone who has read a gripping book about the concentration camps, or someone who has actually visited one, will get a shiver up his spine when this word is mentioned. Then consider how people who have actually been locked up in a concentration camp will feel and react when they hear this word. Perhaps they have tried to protect themselves psychologically by repressing such images and feelings. There are even Germans and Frenchmen who maintain that there never were any concentration camps — the claim that there were is simply a Jewish lie cooked up to support Zionism! And so I conclude that when we talk together about concentration camps, we do not all have the very same thing in mind; rather, each party to the discussion may well be thinking something different — in terms of the reality as well as in terms of how he feels about it.

Take another example — God the Father. For a small child with a fine father, God the Father is also a fine man. The only difference is that God the Father is in heaven and can do *anything,* whereas the child's father on earth has some limits on his powers. But a child with a father who continually mistreats him, who slaps him and kicks him and locks him up in closets and basements, who screams at him and runs him down, so that the child is deathly afraid whenever the father comes home and tries to hide or appear as small as possible — such a child will conceive of God the Father as a tyrant who is even more to be feared than his earthly father. He would not want such a God ever to take notice of him!

When contemporary Christians, under the influence of modern theology, make God the Father into the God who manifests solidarity with us and is one of us, who suffers along with us when we suffer, who does not want us to suffer but is powerless to do anything about it and weeps along with us, they are in effect talking about a different God than other Christians who believe what Lord's Day 42 of the Heidelberg Catechism says about God. Allah, the God worshiped by Muslims, is *one*

— and not triune. For Islam, therefore, there is no God the Son who has made it possible for us to know the Father. Thus the Muslim will say very different things about Allah than the Christian will say about his Father in heaven. If a missionary wants to talk the language of heathen people to whom he is bringing the gospel, he will have to borrow a word for God from *their* language. With that word will come some "content" that is rooted in their way of thinking. Their idea of God may be that He is a power living in a tree or a mountain or an animal, a power with which one must remain on friendly terms — or run the risk of bringing down some misfortune on one's family or tribe. The missionary will have to labor for many years before he can fill their word for God with a different content, such as God the Almighty, the Creator of heaven and earth.

Contradictions between verbal and non-verbal communication

A man visits the eye doctor, and as he steps into his office he proclaims, "I need a new pair of glasses." The doctor says, "Come now, how can you be sure of that even before I have examined you?" The patient says, "I know it, because I can't see what I hear."

The patient is here appealing to a confusing experience people sometimes have: the words they hear do not match the visual signals they receive. Let's suppose a child does something that is not allowed, but it is so funny that you as an adult have difficulty holding back the impulse to laugh. · The child then *hears* that he must immediately stop what he is doing, but what he *sees* on his mother's or father's face is a smile that is only partially concealed. Because non-verbals signals are generally more powerful than verbal ones, there is a good chance that the verbal order to cease will be ignored, while the signal of amusement on the parent's face is followed instead.

Let me give you another example. Praying is speaking respectfully to God. The Lord Jesus often prayed by Himself in the solitude of the wilderness or on a mountain or in a gar-

den. To His disciples He said, "Seek the inner room for prayer."
When we observe how the Pharisees prayed, on the other hand,
we see that the location they chose was not a place apart but
the synagogue or the streetcorner or the open marketplace,
where they were sure to be seen by other people. They even
broadened their phylacteries (Matt. 23:5), again with the intention of being noticed by people. When they prayed, they
beat around the bush, using many words, and in praying for
themselves they did not speak softly but with a loud voice. In
formal terms their prayer was directed to God, but the non-
verbal setting of their prayer was chosen in such a way that
people would be sure to see what outstanding people they were.

Anyone who learns to be attentive to non-verbal signals
will have noticed that although they sometimes confirm and
underscore what is said, they *contradict* it even more often.
Because non-verbal communication is generally taken to be
more reliable than verbal communication (one can lie just as
easily non-verbally as in using words), the chances are that if
there is a *contradiction* between the two, what is *said* will *not*
be accepted as true.

Chapter 6

The Proper Posture for Conversation

*He who gives an answer before he hears, it is folly
and shame to him.*   Prov. 18:13

Everyone knows that a willingness to listen is the first requirement of carrying on a conversation, and many have found
out that it is very difficult to listen. It is difficult especially
because genuine listening involves both the head and the heart.
In this chapter I want to say something not about the heart
but about *conversational conduct,* the kind of conduct that is
visible to both ourselves and others when we are conducting
a conversation. We are not able to look into a person's heart,
and so we do not have the right to say, "Yes, he was present in
body, but his heart was somewhere else." But we can perceive
a person's verbal and non-verbal communication acts and make
judgments about them. For example, one might say, "You in-
terrupted her repeatedly," or, "You kept wringing your hands
in a most irritating way."

Visibly attentive conduct

When you pay careful attention to the words and other
expressions of your conversation partner, it is always possible
for him to note your interest. There are two indicators that
will make this interest apparent to him. The first is that you
assume a *calm, relaxed posture.*

An attitude of calmness in a conversation is indeed the first
requirement. It it not something that is automatically present.
If you are to carry on a conversation, you must take the time for

it. And even if you have properly set some time aside, this does not guarantee that you are calm. Sometimes you may still feel nervous, in which case it would be good to ask yourself what the reason for your nervousness is. Could it be that you are not looking forward to an encounter with your conversation partner? Have you not had sufficient time to get ready? Are you afraid you will not be able to keep yourself under control? Or do you fear you will somehow fail? If there are any such fears or factors in the situation, it is better to pay attention to them before going out to meet your conversation partner. As long as your attention is focused on yourself, you will not be able to fix proper attention on your conversation partner, and he will soon notice this! You will then find yourself becoming tense in an effort to maintain a natural, relaxed posture.

The second indicator of your interest is *eye contact*. In a conversation the two parties normally look at each other. This takes place naturally; it is not a matter of following established rules. Indeed, rules would introduce an element of artificiality here. But if you sit staring at your conversation partner with empty eyes, he will take it as a sign that your attention is on something outside the conversation. On the other hand, you should not lock eyes with your conversation partner either and keep looking directly at him. Such conduct is generally taken as a signal that you are trying to dominate him. But if you keep looking at the ceiling or the walls or the floor, your conversation partner will conclude that you are bored, that you want to terminate the discussion, that you are not interested and perhaps do not know what to say.

Regular eye contact, in which both partners to the conversation can let their glance wander to something else in the room from time to time, is very important. What one sometimes sees in emotional conversations is that a person reacts to what is said by staring out the window or closing his eyes or covering his face with his hands. Perhaps the person who does this when talking with you is ashamed or is trying to mask his tears. You should then wait until the emotional waves subside a bit. A pause in the conversation can be for the good.

Posing open questions

We have already seen that curiosity and suggestive questions and presuppositions are all out of place in a good conversation. How, then, should we conduct ourselves instead?

In general what we should try to do is pose *open questions.* When such questions are asked, the person being addressed can develop an answer in his own way. A closed question instead looks for a yes or a no or some factual item by way of response.

"Are you married?" "What was the date of your wedding?" "Do you have children?" "When were they born?" "Are there no problems with your children?" (Note the suggestive element in this question!) These are examples of closed questions, the kind that make it possible to keep the conversation within certain bounds determined one-sidedly by one of the people in the conversation. What is lamentable about this style of conversation is that the person asking these questions is convinced that he can come up with the *correct* questions, the *relevant* questions. He may well be wrong on this score without even realizing it.

An open question that could be asked in a conversation between a social worker and his client might go as follows: "You have said that there were problems in your marriage. Could I ask you to begin by telling me some things about your marriage in general?" The answer might go something like this: "Yes, I'll try, but it's very difficult for me to talk about it. I really don't know where to begin. Perhaps I should start with the wedding itself. We were married in 1968, when my husband and I were both twenty-one years old ...."

Now, asking open questions is really not all that difficult. The trick is what you do with the answers! Remember that when you ask open questions, you really don't know what you are unleashing. All kinds of thoughts and feelings will come at you from a world of experience that is not your own. Can you handle that? What if you have to deal with events you

abhor, or ideas that are diametrically opposed to all that you
have always stood for foursquare? What will you be asked to
share with your conversation partner? An ocean of misery,
disappointment and folly? Will you come up against someone
who simply *cannot* be comforted, someone living with illusions
that leave you cold? Will you run into bitterness, aggression,
anger, hatred, with some of it directed against yourself and
your good friends? Will you have to deal with utter confusion,
with a person who is at his wit's end, who struggles with very
serious, long-term, unconfessed sins? And what will happen
if you encounter an expansive joy and delight that leaves you
feeling excluded? You just don't know what will come out in
a conversation.

A genuine conversation is and remains a gamble, for it
opens you up to a world that is not your own. You will then
have to deal with the thoughts, feelings and will of your conversation partner, and it is not clear in advance whether you
will be up to it. It may even turn out that your own ideas
are rocked to their foundations. Are you able to "steer" your
emotions in such a way that they do not carry you away? Or
will you repress them, leaving your conversation partner with
the idea that he is dealing with an icicle rather than a warm
human being?

These are the sorts of things you must reckon with when
you win someone's trust by posing open questions and opening
yourself up to any sort of response. But you really have no
choice about the matter. You can try to understand the other
person either on the basis of his or her own life history or
on the basis of a framework of reference you yourself supply,
but you will attain genuine understanding only if your own
experiences, thoughts and feelings largely correspond to those
of your conversation partner.

It can happen that a question unleashes a stream of words;
indeed, even a non-verbal signal is capable of this. And when
such a thing occurs, we are inclined to interrupt — but in most
cases we shouldn't. The stream of words rushing at us is an

emotional release and can be helpful for the further unfolding of the conversation. And so you should try not to get irritated if you sense that your conversation partner is not getting to the point. Perhaps we can learn from a great expert in the art of conversation, who often had people coming to him late in the evening, after he had already gotten undressed, claiming an urgent need to talk with him right then and there. After waiting patiently and listening long enough for the stream of words to end in a trickle, he finally asked, "Is this really what you came here to tell me?" Such a question would then make his conversation partner stop and wonder, "Did I indeed come here to talk about the things I have mentioned so far? Or have I been silent about the real problems? I guess this is the time to speak up." The result was that new words came forth, sometimes many, sometimes only a few, with pauses in between, but as a rule the real problems were then brought to the fore. Usually they were so serious and charged with emotion that they could only be brought up with a listener in whom the speaker had great trust.

If your conversation partner has a long story to tell or has difficulty putting his thoughts into words, perhaps because he is not accustomed to talking about spiritual matters, you can help him along with *small tokens of encouragement.* You can nod occasionally or put an inquiring look on your face or throw in a small word or phrase that is not meant as an interruption but only as a stimulus to keep going in this vein: "Uh-huh. I see what you mean." Of course this is just the sort of thing we are naturally inclined to do.

Verbal attentiveness

Verbal means "with words." The irrefutable proof that you have really been listening is that you pick up on what the other person is saying. It might seem obvious that you would give your attention to what is being discussed, but just try it sometime! Try to hear the words that are spoken and take them in and understand them, recognizing the emotions they embody, and then try to answer in such a way that your conversation partner knows and feels that he has been heard and understood.

You may ask a question and then hardly listen to the answer because you already have another question ready. Why do people fall into this mistake? Perhaps at the very beginning of the conversation you were saying to yourself, "Oh well, this is one of those women who want to liberate themselves." If we start with such a preconception, we will pose a series of suggestive questions in an effort to confirm that opinion, and usually we find the confirmation we wanted because we neatly fish out the answers that fit our pre-established schema.

As soon as our conversation partner has brought up something for discussion, we seize upon it as our opportunity. We offer commentary, often in the form of a value judgment. For example, we might say, "What you're telling me here — you know that it represents a terrible sin, don't you?" Or perhaps we undertake a blocking action: we have our opinion about such a case ready even before we have heard the details. We jump right in and offer our formula, our perspective on the situation.

Interrupting another person when he is talking is seldom the right thing to do — not even when we find our conversation partner long-winded, or when we are irritated at digressions that draw him away from his main point, so that we say to ourselves that he is beating around the bush. In such cases we are often itching to cut our conversation partner off with some such remark as, "Let me sum it up in a few words: for years now you have been perpetrating a fraud," or, "Why don't you hold it right there? I can see just where you're headed."

Fortunately, there are better ways to add an extra dimension to our verbal attentiveness, namely, by arranging the items in our conversation partner's remarks in order, or by summing things up, or by engaging in some reflection on his remarks, or perhaps by using a combination of these three.

Some *sorting out* or ordering may well be needed if the

speaker himself has difficulty putting structure into the story. For example, you might say, "Susan, you have experienced some horrible things, and I can well understand that you find it difficult to tell me about them. At a given moment, when you were about eight years old, you became aware that your mother was regularly beaten by your father. He was so brutal that she wound up in the hospital. Your mother then sought a divorce, with the result that the beatings became even more severe. Finally you ran away, and now, here you sit."

In this example we have both a process of ordering and a *summary* of the story, a story whose telling was punctuated by tearful interruptions. In the summary, the emotional component should be brought to some expression, both verbally and non-verbally.

Reflection really means putting a mirror before someone to let him see himself. We use our own words to try to indicate to our conversation partner what he has been saying to us. Such reflection might begin as follows: "May I put it in my own words? You have ...." Or you might say, "If I have understood you properly ...."

Reflection can have a powerful effect on our conversation partner. If we are on the right track in terms of his emotions and the content of what he is telling us, our reflective comments can be very encouraging to him. He has exerted himself to give us a glimpse of his situation: perhaps he has opened his heart to us. When you reflect his comments back to him accurately, he feels you have understood him, and this gives him satisfaction.

But if you miss the mark in your efforts to reflect or sum up what your conversation partner has told you, you might find him saying something like this: "As far as the main lines are concerned, you have summed me up fairly well ...." But then there comes a correction regarding the part where you went astray. Or perhaps something gets added or clarified, something you did not recognize as sufficiently important to include in your account. But it is also possible that you are told: "I must honestly say that you simply have not understood

me properly." If you get the latter response, you probably have
not listened as well as you should have, in which case you may
have filled in some gaps in your understanding by drawing on
your own experience. The result is that you have not grasped
the heart of the matter, and so you will have to make a new
start!

Listening in a sympathetic and understanding way

When it comes to being verbally attentive, men (in particular) tend to react to what is said in *rational* terms. But the
rational component represents only half of what is there to be
heard. In virtually everything we say there is also an *emotional* component. If you do not pick up on it, you have simply
missed the boat! Now, there are some people who think that
feelings only distort and confuse a conversation. They maintain that when it comes to conversation, you have to go by
reason alone. This is a great misconception, for feelings are
just as much present as thoughts; indeed, it may sound a bit
strange to say it, but they lie even closer to the center of our
personality than thoughts. Our feelings cannot be separated
from ourselves, whereas we have all sorts of thoughts running
through our heads that leave us unmoved because they are not
our thoughts — they do not touch us inwardly.

If you pick up on the ideas being expressed in a conversation but fail to notice the feelings that are present (or perhaps
even denigrate those feelings), your conversation partner will
get the idea that you are not really talking with him or her, and
it will seem as though your mind was on some other matter.
Suppose you have just received word that there was a train accident, with a number of people killed and injured. You might
then talk about it in the following vein: "Now, how is such
a thing possible? Isn't there an automated signal system to
make sure all cars know that a train is approaching?" Perhaps
your conversation partner responds, "No, not all crossings have
such equipment." At that point the telephone rings and you
are told that a member of your family is among those who

were injured in this accident. From that moment on, the train accident is a personal matter for you, something that concerns you very deeply.

To listen in a sympathetic manner (perhaps we could also speak of empathy here) means paying attention to feelings, taking them seriously, and reacting to them. You can show your sympathy in a non-verbal manner, but you can also use words. You might say, "What a tremendous disappointment this must be for you!" Or, "I can see that you're still angry about it." Or, "And now you feel completely wiped out."

When you do this sort of thing, you are embarking on the most difficult aspect of conversation. When people discover that they may express their feelings and have them taken seriously, all sorts of pent-up emotions may suddenly break free, emotions you don't know how to deal with. We cannot very well prescribe in advance how those emotions are to be handled: what you do will depend completely on what kind of person you are, and also on the overall situation, on your relationship to your conversation partner, and on the topic of the conversation. At that point, you should also let your own feelings come out, but not in such a way as to lose control of what you are saying. You will want to take the time that is needed if your conversation partner needs a good cry. In the process you create a sphere of trust, discretion and heartiness.

In the heading above I talked about listening in a sympathetic and *understanding* way. When I speak here of "understanding," I do not just mean a rational comprehension of what the other person is saying. What I am thinking of is our natural tendency to *judge* people.

When we come forward with a negative judgment, we often do so by means of a sentence beginning with "I just don't understand ...." You might say, for example, "I absolutely cannot understand how you could have driven so fast along that road — after all, you know the road like the back of your hand." Or, "What in the world possessed you to suddenly leave your family in the lurch and go and live in a little apartment all by yourself? I just can't understand it." Or, "Is it really *that* difficult for you to leave the bottle alone? I can't imagine why you find that so hard!" Or, "I just don't understand how you could even *consider* getting an abortion!"

The first thing to be observed here is that when a Christian makes such comments to a fellow Christian, he is declaring that such things would be completely out of the question for him. But if this is what he supposes, he does not know himself very well, nor does he acknowledge the great power of sin and temptation. Moreover, such comments block the conversation. All these judgmental remarks are made from within the speaker's own framework of reference. The person who offers such comments is not making a real effort to grasp what moved his conversation partner to act as he did; he is not trying to follow the other person's train of thought or feel his emotions after him.

The effort to listen in an understanding way may be hindered by defensive conduct. Often we are concerned primarily to keep up a good front. And if we do not dare to be genuine, it is because of a fear that our carefully maintained front may crumble. To keep this from happening, we have all sorts of defence mechanisms at our disposal, such as aggression, regression, flight, rationalization, projection, and pretended indifference.

Let's say you are visiting a single person (perhaps a widow or widower) who is confined to bed. You might open the conversation with some such comment as: "Here I am again." Suppose you then get a response like the following: "I wouldn't use that word 'again' if I were you. It was about half a year ago that you were last here, and you promised to come back soon. But half a year slipped by first — I don't call that soon." If we get such a response we are immediately inclined not to accept it, and so we may resort to some defence mechanism, perhaps by saying, "Now, aren't you going a bit too far here? You don't even know why I wasn't able to come, nor do you know all that I went through to make sure you did have some visitors. Or haven't the people I sent been regular in their visits to you?" If you answer this way, you are countering aggression with aggression. Or you might try a different sort of defence mechanism, by saying, "If you only knew how terribly busy I have been, then you would be able to understand that I simply could not come. I certainly was thinking about you, and I did my best to try to get over here, but I couldn't manage it. I just didn't have the time." This defence mechanism is really a form of regression: I, poor and powerless as I am — I just couldn't help it. You might also respond by striking a posture of indifference. Then you first think in your heart, "I'll just let that old complainer whine," and so you say, "Yes, it has been a while since I was here, but let's not lament the fact. We're together now. So how are you doing?"

I'll now leave it to you, the reader, to think of a genuine response, one that doesn't count as a defence mechanism. As you undertake this exercise, assume that what the sick person you are visiting has said is true: you didn't even telephone or send a note or a card. For half a year the person you are visiting heard absolutely nothing from you.

The key to conducting a genuinely helpful conversation in such a situation is to allow yourself to appear imperfect, to let your conversation partner see your faults, and to be aware that he sees them. Then you will not have to hide behind counteraggression or flight or indifference. You will be able to share in the anxieties and sorrows and expectations of your conversation partner, and he will in turn not need to take refuge in aggression or a remote detachment. Instead he will have the feeling that he can speak freely because he is truly being understood.

Unconditional acceptance

The proper posture to take in conversation also involves an unconditional acceptance of the person with whom you are talking. By "unconditional" I mean that you do not lay down requirements in advance. Instead you accept your conversation partner *just as he is.* Thus you do not say to him, "I want to love you, but first you will have to change."

Now, the word "acceptance" could conceivably lead to some misunderstanding. For some people it means approving of that which is unethical and needs to be rejected. I am using the word "acceptance" to mean an acknowledgement of the facts of the matter. If we hope to do something in a situation, we will first have to face up to what is there before us. We will have to accept that there are people who live in a way we completely reject, who do horrible things, who conduct their lives in miserable circumstances that are completely unacceptable from a Christian and social point of view. But Jesus made it clear that Samaritans, unbelievers, whores, tax collectors, blind men, beggars, lepers, people who are possessed by demons, in short, those with whom polite and cultured people would have nothing to do, those who were despised in Jewish society — *they* were precisely the people whom He accepted unconditionally. When Roman soldiers and Samaritans came to John the Baptist, they were sent away, and Jesus was told that He must not eat with Matthew and his friends (Matt. 9:9–13). But the Christ nevertheless accepted the wayward children of the people of Israel, and He also accepted the Samaritans and heathen. This is not to say, of course, that He was thereby approving things that were wrong or wicked. When the Pharisees brought an adulteress to Him, He said: "Neither do I condemn you; go your way; from now on sin no more" (see John 8:1–11).

If God accepted us unconditionally while we were yet sinners (Rom. 5:8), we may also accept our fellow human beings unconditionally. And we can even accept ourselves as we are.

Chapter 7

Second Intermezzo:
Jesus and the Samaritan Woman

> *The Samaritan woman therefore said to Him,
> "How is it that You, being a Jew, ask me for
> a drink since I am a Samaritan woman?" (For
> Jews have no dealings with Samaritans.) Jesus
> answered and said to her, "If you knew the gift of
> God, and who it is who says to you, 'Give Me a
> drink,' you would have asked Him, and He would
> have given you living water."* John 4:9–10

There were four reasons for Jesus *not* to talk with the
Samaritan woman. The first one we read in the text above:
Jews have no dealings with Samaritans. The second had to do
with the time: it was twelve o'clock, the hottest time of the
day. Normally people would eat at this time and then take a
short nap, until the temperature was bearable again. It was
surely not a time for talking. The third was that a rabbi in
Israel did not talk with a woman out in the street, not even
with his own wife or daughter — it was simply contrary to the
customs of the time. Finally, He should not be talking at all
with a woman of questionable morals. And where she stood
morally was evident from the fact that she was at Jacob's well
at noon, when there were *no other women* around.

The Lord Jesus began a conversation with her anyway, and
when the disciples came along, even they were upset by it!
Jesus unconditionally accepted this Samaritan woman, who

was living with a man outside of marriage. Salvation was also intended for her.

The Lord was tired and thirsty, and so He asked for water. This was an everyday request. When the woman indicated that she nevertheless found it a somewhat strange request, Jesus had an opportunity to say that she seemed not to realize with whom she was talking, for if she had any idea of who *He* was, *she* would be asking *Him* for water — indeed, for living water. Here the Lord managed to steer the conversation toward Himself and the work of the Spirit.

For Jews and Samaritans, the term "living water" meant flowing water, water that came from a spring. Because the Samaritans knew the Pentateuch (the five books of Moses) but not the prophets, they would not have understood the expression "living water" in its spiritual sense. A Jew, on the other hand, would quickly have thought of a spiritual meaning, for such meanings were used by the prophets: thus "living water" might stand for the Holy Spirit and His gifts. But the Samaritan woman understood nothing of all this. She was thinking in terms of water one might draw out of a 32-meter deep well, and so she asked, "How can you provide such well water if you have no pail to draw it with? Such a thing could only be done by a very special person — someone greater than our father Jacob."

In His answer Jesus had more to say about that water: "Whoever drinks of the water that I shall give him shall never thirst; but the water that I shall give him shall become in him a well of water springing up to eternal life." The woman's interest in such water was indeed great, for she said, "Sir, give me this water, so I will not be thirsty, nor come all the way here to draw" (4:14–15).

It was evident that the woman had no grasp of the spiritual meaning of "living water," the water that wells up in a person as an everlasting fountain. But the Lord had *two* arrows in His quiver when He began this conversation: what He *was* and what He could *give*. And so He adopted another strategy by getting her to wonder who He was.

"Go, call your husband, and come here." This command caught the Samaritan woman by surprise. She answered with a half truth: "I have no husband." She then got a response from Jesus that showed her how well He was well acquainted with her sinful life. The Samaritan woman was so surprised that a stranger should know these things that she could only draw one conclusion: "Sir, I perceive that You are a prophet" (4:16–19). Jesus had raised the question, "Do you know who it is with whom you are speaking?" She now responded to this question by confessing that He was a prophet. At that moment she did not feel any need to discuss her life further with this prophet, who already knew so much about her. Therefore she undertook a diversionary tactic to draw attention away from herself: the conversation was getting too personal to suit her.. A prophet would surely be interested in an old religious dispute, and so she asked Jesus: "Where are we to worship — in Jerusalem, as the Jews maintain, or here on this mountain, as our fathers have taught us to do?"

In this conversation we have a fine example of *verbal attentiveness.* Anyone who sees through such a diversionary tactic would be inclined to say, "Come now, that's not what we're talking about. Up to now we have been talking about three things — who I am, what I can give you, and what is going on in your life. Let's allow the answer to your question to rest for now and go further with one of these three subjects instead."

But the Lord, who naturally realized that she did not like the personal turn the conversation was taking, chose to respond to her question anyway: "The Jews are right, but the answer is no longer important, for the time has come when it doesn't matter in what place God is worshiped. The true believers — all over the world — will call on the Father in spirit and in truth. Such are the worshipers the Father seeks. God is a Spirit, and those who worship Him must do so in spirit and truth." When Jesus spoke these words, a whole new world opened up before the Samaritan woman. The services in the

temple were no longer necessary, nor were the sacrifices needed
as a foreshadowing of what was to come. The truth itself now
stood revealed. God may be addressed in prayer, but not in
the way a slave speaks to his master; rather, we are to address
Him in the way a child speaks to his father. These were the
worshipers God the Father sought — and *He also wanted her.*
Despite her diversionary tactic, she was back at the original
three subjects in her conversation with Jesus.

The prophet she was talking with got her thinking about
a certain prophecy regarding the Messiah. From the books
of Moses the Samaritans knew that a special prophet was to
come, a prophet who would be greater than Moses and who
would speak the words of God. He would declare all things
to them. The woman wondered whether the time had arrived
when the Messiah, also called Christ, would appear. Jesus
answered her query directly: "He has come. I, who speak
with you, am He." This she believed. She then hurried off to
the city, leaving her water jug behind. She cried out to the
people, "Come with me — I have just met someone who told
me everything I have ever done. Wouldn't he be the Christ?"
This cautious testimony, which was basically an invitation to
people to see for themselves, is the last thing recorded in John's
Gospel regarding Jesus' encounter with the Samaritan woman.

But there are two other conversations in John 4 that have a
bearing on this encounter: one with the returning disciples, and
another with some Samaritans who listened to the woman's
testimony. The conversation with the disciples took place first
of all on a non-verbal level. They saw Jesus talking with a
woman — this struck them as strange. Their amazement could
be read on their faces. Within them arose questions they did
not ask, such as "What are You looking for?" and "Why are
You talking with *her*?" Yet they had their suspicions. In the
meantime, their noon meal of bread was being prepared. The
disciples invited Jesus to eat: "Rabbi, eat." But the Lord did
not eat. The disciples figured that He had not gotten around

to eating while He was talking with the Samaritan woman, yet now He didn't eat either. When the Lord said, "I have food to eat," they began to ask each other, "Could it be that someone has already brought Him some food?" Jesus then proceeded to explain, "My food is to do the will of Him who sent Me, and to accomplish His work" (4:35).

The commission given Him by the one who had sent Him occupied Him so fully that eating and drinking would simply have to wait: after all, the fields were white for harvest. That was the first thing the Lord wants to teach His disciples (and therefore us as well): there are times when the commission given us must take precedence over *everything else*. When we see how the Lord made Himself available for a conversation with a flighty woman that day at noon and then prepared Himself intensely for a further encounter with the Samaritans that afternoon and didn't even take time to eat and drink, we can learn a lesson from the example He set in terms of applying our time and energy to the work of the Kingdom. Our lives should be prime examples of the work of faith and labor of love and steadfastness of hope of which Paul speaks in I Thessalonians 1:3.

The Lord gives His disciples some instruction about that steadfastness of hope. Through the green fields the Samaritans were approaching. Now, the harvest time was still far away, but Jesus said to the disciples, "The fields are white for harvest." He also declared, "In this case the saying is true, 'One sows, and another reaps'" (4:37). This proverb is generally taken as expressing a somber thought, but the Lord uses it in a positive way here. In nature there are usually some months between sowing and harvest. If no catastrophe takes place, the person who sowed the seed can presumably gather in the harvest. But in spiritual life it doesn't always go quite so smoothly, for sometimes there are years — even centuries — between sowing and harvest. The Samaritans knew the books of Moses and they were aware that the great prophet was to come. That much had already been sown. Perhaps they had heard John the Baptist preach that the time was drawing near and that they had to be converted. But Jesus, the Messiah who had now come, proceeded to gather in the harvest. He remained in Sychar for two days, and many came to believe His word — and even progressed beyond the disciples, who were still thinking that Jesus would establish a kingdom of *Israel*. The Samaritans now said, "We know that this One is indeed the Savior of *the world*."

This lesson is of great importance for all who must carry on a spiritual conversation with believers who are falling away, or with unbelievers. If the harvest is not to be reaped by the one who sowed, there still remains the commission to continue with the sowing, for God, in His own good time, will give the increase.

Chapter 8

The Proper Attitude to Take

We give thanks to God always for all of you, mak-
ing mention of you in our prayers; constantly
bearing in mind your work of faith and labor of
love and steadfastness of hope in our Lord Jesus
Christ in the presence of our God and Father.

I Thess. 1:2–3

The heart

In a previous chapter I wrote about the proper *postures* and *attitudes* for conversation. At that point I limited myself to those aspects of our conduct which our conversation partner is able to perceive. But now I want to turn to what goes on *within,* i.e. which is not visible when we engage in conversation. Our inner attitudes, flowing from the heart as the center of our personality, determine our conduct to quite an extent.

Anyone who wants to talk about salvation will have to be a partaker of salvation himself. Through the proclamation of the gospel, the Holy Spirit brings about in our hearts the work of faith and labor of love and steadfastness of hope. What God has wrought within us will become visible in our conduct, in what we do and refrain from doing. The Christian will manifest the form of Christ because he is renewed in the image of his Savior.

Faith

> *Now faith is the assurance of things hoped for,*
> *the conviction of things not seen.* Hebrews 11:1

The works of faith are the proclamation and spreading of God's Name. The response to such proclamation is that His Name is confessed in doctrine and in life.

In everyday life we encounter both believers and unbelievers among our fellow human beings. In our encounters with people at home and in the church, at work and in our recreation, we get into many conversations. Some of those conversations we have arranged by appointment, but there are also many that spring up without prior planning. In those spontaneous conversations, which we may have with either friends or strangers, our works of faith must be made manifest, for it is our heartfelt desire to love the Lord our God and to serve Him according to His Word. We want to say "Yes" and "Amen" to that Word. Therefore it is not really possible for someone who suffers from doubt to talk about salvation in Christ. Doubt makes us uncertain. James says: "But let him ask in faith without any doubting, for the one who doubts is like the surf of the sea driven and tossed by the wind. For let not that man expect that he will receive anything from the Lord, being a double-minded man, unstable in all his ways" (James 1:6–8).

Doubt has very serious consequences. Anyone who doubts what God says, who doubts His love and power, will hardly be able to pray. How in the world is such a doubter supposed to pray with and for others?

All believers fight a battle against the weakness of their own faith. But where the battle against doubt and unbelief is really being fought, the LORD teaches us again and again to say "Amen" to His Word.

The labor of love

> *For the love of Christ controls us, having con-*
> *cluded this, that one died for all, therefore all*
> *died; and He died for all, that they who live*
> *should no longer live for themselves, but for Him*
> *who died and rose again on their behalf.*
>
> II Cor. 5:14–15

When the love of Christ constrains us, with the result that we talk about the one Mediator who gave His life as a ransom for many, then we are serving Him and our neighbor (and not ourselves) by speaking. Yet I can well imagine that deep in our hearts we are happy to be praised for the help we have given or the fine conversation we have conducted. In and of itself this is not wrong, but anyone who knows himself well will realize how quickly we are inclined to seek the honor for ourselves. The determination to think less of ourselves than of others, and not to put on airs, and to be ready to perform any labor of love, even if there is no honor to be gained thereby — such a determination is not ours by nature. If we are sometimes able to act out of love, it is because we wish to return love to the one who first loved us. Such love manifests itself when we keep His commandments and listen to His Word (see John 14:15 and 13:23). Such love is also evident when we try to serve God in the conversations we conduct, in an effort to love God and our neighbor.

The steadfastness of hope

> *But sanctify Christ as Lord in your hearts, al-*
> *ways being ready to make a defense to every one*
> *who asks you to give an account for the hope that*
> *is in you, yet with gentleness and reverence; and*
> *keep a good conscience so that in the thing in*

which you are slandered, those who revile your
good behavior in Christ may be put to shame.

I Peter 3:15–16

"Faith" and "hope" are words that suggest a measure of
uncertainty when used in everyday life. One might say, "I
believe it, but I can't really be sure," or, "We'll just have to
hope for the best — we may be pleasantly surprised, but we
may also be disappointed." In the Bible it works just the other
way around, for faith and hope have to do with present and
future certainties that are given us in God's reliable promises.
Thus Peter speaks of the hopeless situation after the death of
Jesus, when things seemed to have run dead, and he also speaks
of the living hope the disciples possessed once Jesus had risen
from the dead.

Their hope had to do with regeneration, whereby we receive, as grace in Christ, the forgiveness of sins, the resurrec-
tion of the body and the life everlasting — all of this as an
inheritance which God has laid away for His children. It is an
imperishable inheritance that cannot spoil or decay; it cannot
be stained or lose its beauty in some other way. It is an untar-
nished inheritance that never fades away or loses its value and
luster.

We may testify of this hope, and we must always be prepared to give an account of it. We have an opportunity to
do so when we conduct spiritual conversations. Therefore our
manner of speaking must be in agreement with our holy walk
of life and with a clear conscience. When we give an account
of the hope that is in us, we may be bold, but at the same time
we must be modest, gentle and reverent.

This hope gives us the power to disregard ourselves. When
we consider carefully what *we* are, we cannot understand why
God would want to use people like us as instruments to speak
for Him and to spread His Word. But when we keep an eye on
that imperishable inheritance, we learn to relativize ourselves
in a healthy way. God is building a house, and when He is

finished, there will not be a single stone missing. As for ourselves, we know that we continually fall short of the mark, also when we speak about the Savior and His gifts. Naturally, this is not an excuse for laziness or stupidity or laxness or lovelessness on our part. On the other hand, it may comfort us to remember these assurances when we fail to carry on a good conversation with someone, even though we prepared carefully and tried hard. At present we still live in a state of sin and brokenness, or temptation and distress.

God's promises are yes and amen. One day all the children of the heavenly Father will speak and sing perfectly.

Chapter 9

Contrary Voices

> *But as for me, my feet came close to stumbling;*
> *My steps had almost slipped.*
> *For I was envious of the arrogant,*
> *As I saw the prosperity of the wicked.*
> *When I pondered to understand this,*
> *It was troublesome in my sight*
> *Until I came into the sanctuary of God;*
> *Then I perceived their end.*
>
> Psalm 73:2–3, 16–17

A complaint against God

Perhaps some readers of the previous chapter could already hear a voice of protest arising within their hearts. Thus the voice that speaks of our faith and love and hope may be countered by an opposing voice that asks some questions and may even *contradict* the original voice. Think of what Asaph said to himself: "I almost slipped and fell, for when I pondered matters, I looked upon the godless with disfavor and was troubled." And Asaph was not the only one to hear such a contrary voice welling up from within.

David said: "O my God, I cry by day, but Thou dost not answer; and by night, but I have no rest" (Ps. 22:2). He also cried out: "To Thee, O LORD, I call; my Rock, do not be deaf to me, lest, if Thou be silent to me, I become like those who go down to the pit" (Ps. 28:1). In Psalm 44 the sons of Korah sang about Israel's God and King, who did mighty deeds for His people. Yet they also declared: "Thou hast rejected us and

56

brought us to dishonor. Thou dost make us a reproach to our neighbors. Arouse Thyself, why dost Thou sleep, O LORD? Awake, do not reject us forever. Why dost Thou hide Thy face, and forget our affliction and our oppression?" (vs. 9, 13, 23–24). We also think of Job (see Chapter 11 below) and of the many pious people in the Old and New Testaments who cried out to God from earnest temptations, even though they felt God was not listening.

How often God's children today raise the same lament, which sometimes grows into an accusation! Why, O God, have You led us down this path? Why does this catastrophe strike us? Why do Your beloved children have to suffer this? Why do Your people and Your church find themselves in this predicament? Why all these divisions and conflicts, why this half-heartedness and falling away? These are all questions for which we will not get an answer as long as we suppose, in our pride, that we have the *right* to an answer. Sometimes we are so rebellious that for a long time the voice of rebellion issues from our lips, throttling the voice of faith.

God's plan for this world has shocked many Christians. In the second world war, millions of people perished in extermination camps like Auschwitz. Today there are wars that drag on and on: we see entire villages being wiped out with chemical weapons. Hundreds of thousands of children die in hunger and misery not long after they are born. Even so, we sing that God is powerful above all others, and that the whole world bows before Him and admires His works.

A complaint against ourselves

The contrary voice is also sounded from an entirely different corner. We hear it as a complaint directed not against God but against ourselves.

If I am called on to testify, to talk to others about the salvation that is ours in Christ, how can I possibly do so when I take a good look at myself, at *my* weak faith, *my* doubts, *my* temptations? How can I testify if my conscience speaks up at the same time and asks me: "Do you stand fully behind what you are saying? Are you being honest — or hypocritical? How is your own battle against sin faring? And how about your prayer life?" Doubts may well arise about how far we have come, especially when we think of what Paul says: "I have fought the good fight, I have finished the course, I have kept the faith; in the future there is laid up for me the crown of righteousness, which the Lord, the righteous Judge, will award to me on that day; and not only to me, but also to all who have loved His appearing" (II Tim. 4:7–8).

A contrary voice from the world

There is another way for the contrary voice to launch a counterattack. The angle of approach is then the world around us. This world does not remain silent but speaks with a powerful voice about its wants and desires, paying no attention to God or to moral rules. We see a science that denies God and a powerful technology that renders the Almighty superfluous. We even come upon Biblical scholarship that rids itself of the notion of the Bible as the inspired Word of God, and a morality that is derived from the desires of godless men. These trends press upon us so insistently that we can hardly get around them. Think, for example, of how our eyes and ears are constantly assaulted by stimuli aiming to arouse our sexual desires. The satisfaction of our lusts has become the central goal to be achieved in many sectors of society.

This contrary voice can even lead to contrary behavior. Think of the various forms of enslavement in which people become entangled. I think of the slavery of drugs, of smoking, of eating or snacking, of sexual desires, of wasteful spending, of gambling, of sports and recreation, of reading and watching television. And then there are people who are slaves to their work, and people who seek recognition and status above all. These, and other forms of slavery which I have not mentioned, are all indications that the voice of God is not being heard or is rendered powerless in the lives of certain people.

A positive contrary voice

It is clear that when we hear the contrary voice, we must often judge it in negative terms as the voice of our deadly enemy, the Devil, and as the voice of the world and of our own flesh (Heidelberg Catechism, Lord's Day 52). But there is also a contrary voice that is bound up with believing, a believing that has not yet become sight. It is a voice of need, of spiritual longing, of forsakenness, of desire. This contrary voice, which drives us toward the "holy place," to the administration of God's Word and sacraments, sends us into our inner room where we can call on God in prayer and study His Word in faith.

These are the means God provides for us, also when we are tempted and tried by our deadly enemies. Therefore, when each day we raise the prayer expressed in the sixth petition of the Lord's Prayer, we may ask for the power of the Holy Spirit so that we will not lose the spiritual battle but remain standing — indeed, fight back mightily and triumph eventually.

The contrary voice in conversation

The contrary voice has great significance in our conversations with others. I have mentioned a number of tools God provides for our use in the spiritual battle. We must add that our conversation partner can be a great help in strengthening us and encouraging us for the battle of faith. And here is something of the greatest importance: we can be sure that our conversation partner has heard the contrary voice speaking in his own heart. Therefore he will know what we are talking about. Instead of thinking such thoughts as, "What a doubter! What a sinful life! What a weakling!" he will say to himself, "I, too, am still inclined to all sorts of evil deeds." Then we can talk about the struggle we went through before we were able to make our voice heard again. Such openness can show us the way in a conversation with someone who does not see the way himself or does not have the power to walk in it.

The contrary voice can also take the upper hand. When this happens in our lives, we are not in a position to be of help to others. We first have to be helped ourselves.

When the contrary voice takes complete control of our conversation partner, we hear some frightening things. Nothing more is said about being engaged in a dialogue with God. Instead we hear about rejection, about contact that has been broken off, about an inability to pray, about a complete deadening when it comes to spiritual matters, about total indifference. Feelings of loathing and hatred are expressed in relation to God and the church. We hear complaints about loveless and hypocritical Christians, and about unfaithful office-bearers. Sometimes there was indeed something in the conduct of elders and office-bearers and church members to give rise to such talk. Perhaps something took place that was so dreadful that we can only be ashamed of it, making no effort whatever to justify or explain it.

If you are involved in such a conversation, you must be extremely careful. You should then pray that God, with His Spirit, will help you find just the right words. And you must trust in His promises.

Chapter 10

Presuppositions and Value Judgments

Jesus said to him, "I am the way, and the truth, and the life; no one comes to the Father, but through Me."   John 14:6

And there is salvation in no one else; for there is no other name under heaven that has been given among men, by which we must be saved.
Acts 4:12

There are many matters about which we have a fixed opinion. We don't have to think about them: our mind is already made up. We have drawn our conclusion at some earlier point in life. When we think about a problem, we are fortunate to have such examples ready to hand so that we can proceed from them as fixed givens.

For example, we do not need to wonder what would happen if we had something in our hand and then let it go. We know in advance that it would fall. This is a judgment we have derived from our life's experience. Perhaps we heard something about the theory behind this judgment in a science class when we were taught about the law of gravity.

Many of our presuppositions derive from science. Probably all of us believe that matter is composed of molecules, and that the molecules are in turn made up of atoms involving a nucleus and some electrons.

Last but not least, there are presuppositions grounded in our existential convictions, especially our Christian beliefs. One such Christian presupposition can be found in the two texts quoted at the beginning of this chapter. This presupposition is of far-reaching importance in our conversations with non-Christians. We sometimes encounter people with whom we are very impressed, people who live by high moral standards, who struggle against injustice, oppression and poverty. We value and respect such people for how they live — and yet we must say that they do not know the way that leads to life.

We import our presuppositions into life situations, and so we arrive at value judgments. At times we say of the opinions people hold, or of the conduct they engage in, or even of the people as such, that they are good or bad, correct or wrong, secure or insecure, holy or godless, valuable or worthless.

Now we can see that there are two ways to go wrong when it comes to conversations. One way is to rely on presuppositions that are not correct, and the other is to fail to assess the situation properly.

When Mesha, the king of Moab, was making war on King Jehoram of Israel and King Jehoshaphat of Judah, he realized at a certain point that the battle was going against him. He tried to break out but failed. He then decided to sacrifice his beloved first-born son, who was supposed to succeed him on the throne, as a sacrifice to his god Chemosh. It was a presupposition grounded in his faith that brought him to this horrible deed, and that faith was confirmed by the result, for the Israelites did withdraw (see II Kings 3:25–27).

We believe that God does not want human sacrifices, but that He has given up His own Son as an atonement for all our sins. Therefore we would not act as Mesha did if we were in a comparable situation. Yet we, too, need to guard against appealing to value judgments which we claim glibly to have gotten from the Bible.

At a Reformed Ladies' Society meeting a member declared, "Because I find so little satisfaction in doing my housework, I am thinking about taking a job outside the house." She was startled when she was told that what she wanted was sinful and wrong: she would be setting a bad example for other women, for the Bible teaches that a woman belongs in her home and must find work to do there. The presupposition she expressed was not really derived from the Bible but came from a social state of affairs which had been taken as a model by the working classes, the merchants and the farmers, who did not think that a woman should limit herself to the work of the household at all. I could also give many examples from the past to illustrate that value judgments really were expressed (e.g. about sports) on the basis of Bible texts. If you read the conversations of Job with his friends (see Chapter 11), you will see that the three friends had a rather fixed view of how God acts. Their presupposition grounded in faith was completely off target — so much so that God became very angry at Eliphaz and the two other men and told them they would have to make a sacrifice and get Job to pray for them.

It can also happen that we misjudge a situation and therefore arrive at a value judgment that misses the mark. We can find examples of this as well in the book of Job. We become guilty of this error when we announce our conclusion on a matter before we have properly understood the situation. Perhaps our conversation partner has not yet had an opportunity to have his full say.

We seem to feel an urgent need to arrive quickly at a value judgment when it comes to the affairs of others. Think of David, who said, "Surely the man who has done this deserves to die." But Nathan shot back, "You are the man!" (II Sam. 12) There are various kinds of judgments we are inclined to utter which, as a rule, do not get us anywhere but rather block genuine progress: "That's a very serious sin!" and "You took on a tremendous burden of guilt by doing that" and "You can't be depended on" and so forth. The person at whom we hurl such judgments will then steer clear of us — but not because he isn't aware of his own sin and guilt. The problem is rather that he is all too aware of it and must somehow deal with it.

It is quite understandable that there are people who say, "If you want to talk in a genuine and open way with people, you must set your presuppositions aside for a while." Now, if you really believe the texts quoted at the beginning of this chapter, which proclaim that there is only one Savior, Jesus Christ, and only one way to salvation, then why would you want to engage in conversation with Christians who have fallen away, or with Jews or Muslims, or with people who don't claim to belong to any religious tradition at all? The problem is precisely that although it is possible to remain silent about what you really think and to find out all about the faith (or unbelief) of your conversation partner, eventually you will have to come clean regarding your own purpose and intent. A very sensible question that may be asked of you is this: "What are your real reasons for wanting to talk with me (or with us)? Is it for evangelistic motives?" You cannot honestly answer this question with a No. A second obvious and unavoidable question is this: "If we are to talk with you and listen to you and believe what you say, is it also possible that you will listen to us in such a way that *we* convince *you* of our faith (or unbelief) and lead you to adopt *our* outlook on life?" This question we would have to answer with a forthright No. If we were to say Yes, if we really believed it was possible for us to come to different convictions through such a conversation or to turn into unbelievers, we would be denying the Savior.

Presuppositions grounded in faith are indeed obstacles to a completely open approach in a conversation. Such conversations are certainly far from simple. But the love of Christ sends us forward, and we are led by God's Word and Spirit.

There are also value judgments of an entirely different sort that require our attention here because they can influence our conversations in a far-reaching way. I am thinking of the value judgments we form about people.

We all know (or sometimes say we know) that black people are lazy, that Jews are gifted but unreliable, that people with such-and-such an ethnic background are stubborn, that city people like to show off and are glib talkers, that farmers are stupid, that people who live in trailers are probably gypsies, that gypsies are thieves, and so forth. If you get involved in an intense relationship with someone from one of these groups about which you have such value judgments sitting ready at the tip of our tongue, you will occasionally have your value judgment confirmed. There are, after all, some lazy black people. But if you are honest about it — and this can cause you pain and trouble at times — you will have to admit that there are very industrious, hard-working black people as well, and you will wind up wondering whether there is really any difference between white people and black people in this regard.

Anyone who thinks this discussion does not apply to him because he has no contact with people in any of these categories fails to realize that we also wind up applying such value judgments to people on an individual basis as we deal with them in ordinary life. Sometimes we ground such presuppositions in earlier experience ("Anyone who steals once is always a thief") or in what other people have told us ("Always be on guard when you are dealing with him"). We are probably inclined to view certain members of our own congregation as saints, whereas there are others on whose heads we almost expect to see horns sprouting.

It should be obvious by now that such value judgments, most of which are negative, have the effect of blocking progress in a conversation. They make it impossible for us to listen in a genuinely receptive manner. The remedy for this situation is obvious: we must become conscious of such presuppositions and of how they affect us in conversation. Are we inclined to view our conversation partner in a certain light? Do we tend to think of him (or her) in largely negative terms? If so, why? If we are able to get beyond such presuppositions without automatically focusing on negative features we think we see, remarkable things will start to happen. We will encounter an entirely different person!

Chapter 11

Third Intermezzo:
Job and His Distant Friends

> *O that you would be completely silent, and that*
> *it would become your wisdom!* Job 13:5

The book of Job includes entire conversations that took place between Job and his friends Eliphaz, Bildad and Zophar. Later Elihu entered the discussion. In these conversations we see examples of verbal and non-verbal communication, which illustrate some of the points made in previous chapters. The example of Job and his friends gives us some illustrations of what often happens in conversations. Because these conversations are recorded for us in the Bible, I propose to look at them to see what they can teach us about conversational techniques.

Perhaps you were struck by the word "distant" in the title of this chapter. The first thing we note is that Job had been forsaken by the members of his family (think of what his wife said to him) and by friends who lived nearby. Job says, "He has removed my brothers far from me, and my acquaintances are completely estranged from me. My relatives have failed, and my intimate friends have forgotten me" (19:13–14). Job had expected that his relatives and closest friends would be the first ones to look him up and offer him comfort, but he waited in vain. We read that he waited for *months* (7:3), but his relatives and close friends did not come. Why not? We can only guess.

The conduct of those who should have surrounded Job with their love and concern is very much like our own when we have to respond to some dramatic event in our circle of family and friends, or when we must act as office-bearers. Let us suppose that the father of a young family is struck dead by lightning, or that a whole family except for one child is killed in an automobile accident, with the surviving child seriously and permanently injured, or that the mother of a large family becomes ill and there is no healing possible. We are all familiar with such horrible situations, and if we have to get involved ourselves, we often do not know what to say. If we are to offer comfort, we will want to say something about what God means to accomplish through this suffering. But what if we are like Job in that we simply cannot understand but can only be thankful that God is wise in all His doings? Then we are left with the feeling that we really have nothing to say. The result is that we stay away entirely, just when our presence could bring so much comfort to the afflicted.

The family and close friends did not show up to comfort Job. But the news of the misfortune that had struck Job traveled to faraway lands, where it was heard by some of his distant friends. Those friends talked it over and decided to make a trip together to commiserate with Job and comfort him (2:11). When they finally approached Job after their long journey, the situation turned out to be much grimmer than they had heard: Job was covered with horrible boils, and they did not recognize him until they were very close to him. The sight of Job frightened and amazed them so much that they could not utter a word. Yet, without using language they were able to manifest their sympathy and sorrow: in the manner of the ancient Near East, they cried aloud and wept. They tore their clothes and threw dust in the air, which then descended on their head and their clothes. These were heartfelt *gestures* by which they demonstrated that Job's suffering and sorrow was also theirs. They did not use words. They were simply dumbfounded when they saw how great Job's pain was (2:13).

Commentators have not always agreed in their judgment of this conduct on the part of the three friends. Some have

described the seven days and nights of silence in Job's presence
as a new trial for the poor man to endure: it was enough to
drive Job mad. But others have spoken of the seven days
of silence in positive terms: as long as the three friends kept
silent, Job could draw some comfort from their presence and
their lamentation as they joined him in his suffering. It was
only when they opened their mouths and began to talk that
things took a horrible turn!

I do not endorse either of these approaches. If you are
comforting a friend who is suffering as Job did but have never
suffered in such a way yourself, there is only one thing to do:
show that you share your friend's suffering by simply seeking
him out, by being with him. Words do not help much at such
a time. The sufferer is still reeling from the shock of what
has befallen him; he has to realize the extent and depth of his
plight. This is a process that takes some time. If you enter
such a situation with words, you may quickly be perceived as
someone who does not realize the depth of human suffering.
You may have the best of intentions when you offer comfort
by quoting some Bible text, but is this a genuine response on
your part? Isn't it a little like putting a bandage on a wound
that is still bleeding?

Thus we can have some appreciation for the silence of the
three friends — at least at the beginning. They were trying to
understand how Job must be feeling, and they were considering
what to say to him. But something went wrong. In all their
reflection they did not come up with anything they could say
meaningfully. And so they remained silent until their silence
became an obsession, a fresh torment for the righteous Job.
The silence of the three friends became so oppressive that it
was finally Job himself who broke it — by cursing the day of
his birth. Why does God allow people to be born if misfortune
and suffering are their lot in life? Why not die a quick death?
"If only I had never been born!" lamented Job. "And if I could
only die, I would have rest."

Then Eliphaz asked for permission to say something: "If

one ventures a word with you, will you become impatient?"
(4:2) Naturally Job expected that his friends, after considering
the matter for such a long time, would have some wise, comforting words for him. Unfortunately, Eliphaz's fear turned out
to be well founded: Job grew impatient with their words, for
they caused him sorrow and pain.

Eliphaz made a particularly inept beginning. He started
with the following presupposition: someone who knows how to
offer encouragement to others should also be able to encourage himself. Therefore he said: "Behold, you have admonished
many, and you have strengthened weak hands. Your words
have helped the tottering to stand, and you have strengthened
feeble knees. But now it has come to *you,* and you are impatient; it touches *you,* and you are dismayed" (4:3–5). Note
that Eliphaz begins with high praise for Job. But from this
presupposition he arrives at the following negative value judgment: "Job, I'm disappointed in you. If you managed to help
so many people out of the pit, why can't you do more to encourage yourself?"

Even the most steadfast believer in the world would be
amazed if all those misfortunes struck him! Moreover, Eliphaz
is not correct in presupposing that someone who is able to
comfort others should also be able to comfort and encourage
himself. When it comes to shocking experiences like the ones
Job underwent, there is a long process of working through the
material, a process that involves denial, regression and aggression, resignation and taking fresh courage. This process can
take months — even years.

Eliphaz's negative value judgment about Job's conduct can
be explained on the basis of his mistaken reading of the situation. Perhaps Job would still have been able to comfort himself
if at that moment he really believed what he had undoubtedly
proclaimed to others, namely, that the Lord is with us even
when we suffer and undergo reversals. But Job wrestled with
the question: Why does God oppose me? Why has He cut off
every avenue of escape? These frightful thoughts tormented

him day and night.

As Eliphaz continued to speak, we come upon a second pre-supposition he was working with, one which we are tempted to regard as grounded in *faith*. Eliphaz and his friends assumed that people who serve God faithfully also encounter misfortune, sorrow and sickness on occasion, but that it will surely disappear from their lives again because God rewards a righteous walk of life. Therefore Eliphaz said: "Is not your fear of God your confidence, and the integrity of your ways your hope? Remember now, who ever perished being innocent? Or where were the upright destroyed?" (4:6–7) And so, Job, there's no need for you to sit here in sackcloth and ashes; if you had really been living a pious life, this suffering would have passed before long.

Eliphaz was working with a pair of connected faith presuppositions: if the suffering does not go away after a while, and if it is as serious as in the case of Job, then Job must not be the righteous man we took him to be. And so Eliphaz concluded that Job was being punished for grave sins! The three friends became ever more convinced that Job was not a righteous man but a *hypocrite* who was guilty of some very serious sins. This was a devastating value judgment about Job's life. In order to persuade Job that they were right, Eliphaz finally went to far as to say: "Is it because of your reverence that He reproves you, ,that He enters into judgment against you? Is not your wickedness great, and your iniquities without end? For you have taken pledges of your brothers without cause, and stripped men naked. To the weary you have given no water to drink, and from the hungry you have withheld bread. But the earth belongs to the mighty man, and the honorable man dwells in it. You have sent widows away empty, and the strength of the orphans has been crushed" (22:4–9).

Now, we know that Job was upright and pious, that he feared God and avoided evil (1:1). Thus when we hear Eliphaz utter such horrible accusations, we are inclined to say: "How in the world does he come to such conclusions?" He could never have *heard* this sort of thing about Job. His value judgment that Job was a hypocritical sinner was grounded in his own mistaken presupposition. Eliphaz was reasoning backwards: Job was being punished (he thought), and so he must have committed some grave sins. Moreover, it was clear that Job was not about to stop protesting and declaring his innocence. His stubbornness made the situation all the more difficult, for he would not ask for forgiveness either. Therefore the three friends would have to put pressure on him, and perhaps use some harsh means. And so Eliphaz began uttering accusations: Job had gotten rich at the expense of the poor and powerless. He had conducted himself like an oppressor without a conscience. Eliphaz would have to accuse Job openly, in the hope that Job would then make a clean breast of it. That's why we find Eliphaz coming forward with such *suggestive presuppositions.*

Three times Eliphaz expressed a negative value judgment about Job, and the charges he brought against him were by no means minor or trivial. Even though the presuppositions he started with were grounded in faith or belief, they were mistaken. Eliphaz, Bildad and Zophar talked about God in terms people must use if they are trying to understand Him and calculate His actions. Their schema was that God rewards the righteous and punishes the godless. In that schema there was no place for the realization that God *tests* believers, or for the recognition that great sinners can sometimes be unbelievably prosperous (see Ps. 73), even when they oppress, persecute and kill the faithful. In all of this the three friends did not speak rightly of God.

If we now try to imagine how Job must have felt about the things his three friends said to him, we soon realize that they made his suffering even worse. Their intention to bring Job some comfort came to nought, and Job cried out: "Sorry comforters are you all." They laid very serious accusations on the table, and they persisted with their charges because Job did not want to give in and admit they were right. This righteous man, at the end of his tether, finally said, "Pity me, pity me, O you my friends" (19:21). But he found no pity among people, and so he appealed to God: "As for me, I know that my Redeemer lives, and at the last He will take His stand on the earth. Even after my skin is flayed, yet without my flesh I shall see God" (19:25–26).

Elihu, who was involved in this situation as a fourth friend, took a different attitude. He placed himself *next to Job,* for he declared, "Behold, I belong to God like you; I too have been formed out of the clay. Behold, no fear of me should terrify you, nor should my pressure weigh heavily on you" (33:6–7). Furthermore, Elihu was not trapped in the schema the other friends were using, for he said, "God speaks to people in various different ways. No human being is able to say to God that he is righteous. Every person stands guilty before God. But neither is any human being able to discharge his debt before God." Elihu then told the story of a person who was deathly ill but was suddenly healed because something miraculous happened:

> If there is an angel as mediator for him,
> One out of a thousand,
> To remind a man what is right for him,
> Then let him be gracious to him, and say,
> "Deliver him from going down to the pit,
> I have found a ransom" (33:23–24).

That was the joyful message Elihu brought: God is not your enemy, as you may think. The LORD is your friend!

The Book of Job has shown us how people with the best of intentions are sometimes unable to offer genuine comfort, how they wind up robbing the children of God of the last little bit of light instead of helping them. This can happen because of mistaken presuppositions and schemas.

The Pharisees did the same thing. They used infallible schemas to make the law applicable to daily life. They could distinguish between good and bad even in the most trivial cases. But in the process they wound up rendering God's law powerless as far as its real purpose is concerned. They laid burdens on the people which God did not intend them to bear. They, too, were without mercy. They did not want to live on the basis of mercy but instead tried to earn everything by their own merit. They were the righteous ones who had no need of Jesus Christ as the Savior. And they became furious when they were unmasked by Christ as people who would be lost if they did not believe in Him. Their schemas meant more to them than the Light of the World.

When you are judging a person or his conduct or a situation, you should first ask yourself what presuppositions you are relying on. It may well be that your presuppositions are not absolute and unchangeable truths!

Chapter 12

Leading a Conversation

> *And He said to them, "O foolish men and slow of heart to believe in all that the prophets have spoken! Was it not necessary for the Christ to suffer these things and to enter into His glory?" And beginning with Moses and with all the prophets, He explained to them the things concerning Himself in all the Scriptures.*
>
> Luke 24:25–27

Two disappointed men were walking from Jerusalem to Emmaus. They were engrossed in conversation, *exchanging ideas* about all that had happened. The one offered this suggestion, the other that, and they took turns addressing questions to each other. It was a conversation in which they shared as equals and listened attentively to one another. The two friends watched jointly over the progress of the conversation. Now, one would expect that they could bring some clarity to the problem they were discussing, and that they would work it out together. Yet the opposite took place. The more they talked about it, the more incomprehensible the whole business became. They simply could not figure out what was going on with Jesus of Nazareth.

A man approached on foot and joined them. At first He listened to their conversation, but soon He joined in and posed an (open) question: "What are these words you are exchanging with one another as you are walking?" The two men were amazed at this question. They even stood still as they delivered their answer. From the somber looks on their faces it was apparent that they were not talking about the weather or the landscape but about a matter that meant a great deal to them. Didn't this stranger know what had been going on in Jerusalem with Jesus of Nazareth? Another (open) question came their way: "What things?" And now something interesting happened: the stranger met with a response, and from that moment on He led the conversation. Yet this did not mean that *He* did all the talking: the two men journeying to Emmaus first gave an expansive account of the recent events. Leading a conversation does not mean that you are the only one who says anything; rather, you must see to it that the rights of your conversation partner(s) get respected.

It is also striking that a certain intimacy and trust had already been established, for the two men spoke openly of the hope that was within them, namely, that this Jesus would be the one who was to deliver Israel. It may well be that the stranger spoke in a manner which revealed that He knew everything they had been saying, for He addressed them in a very personal way. He even confronted them with a value judgment: "O foolish men and slow of heart to believe in all that the prophets have spoken!"

When you are confronted with a value judgment like that, you must either refute it or accept it. How in the world could the stranger have come to such a conclusion? He proceeded to explain it to them. But first he gave them a summary: the Christ had to suffer in order to enter into His glory. Then He backed up His summary and conclusion by reference to the Scriptures. The two men traveling to Emmaus certainly knew well enough what Moses and the prophets had said, but as for the passages that had to do with a suffering messiah, they had ignored them, just as the other Jews had done. Now Jesus took the same "information" they had access to and placed it in the proper light, so that it took on a whole new significance! This confused them utterly. If these things were true, Jesus of Nazareth was the Messiah, the Redeemer, after all! Their hearts burned as the Scriptures were opened for them.

I have told the story of the two men traveling to Emmaus in a little different manner in order to bring out certain aspects having to do with conversational leadership. Obviously, exercising leadership in a conversation is an aspect of leadership in general. Thus what we are talking about here is the development of certain talents for leadership. What are those talents?

When you are a leader, you have certain *goals* you hope to attain together with another person or persons. The parties to the conversation must be one or become one about the purpose of their conversation. If they do not attain unity, at least one of them will feel disappointed when the conversation is over. In our example of the two men traveling to Emmaus, the risen Christ's goal was to make the two men, who regarded His death as a catastrophic defeat, realize that the Christ *had* to suffer in order to enter His glory. He wanted them to understand that it was a great fact of redemptive history.

Someone who assumes leadership must also *take initiatives.* It was certainly no accident that the Lord got involved in a conversation with Clopas and the other man (who may well have been Luke). *Christ* took the initiative in bringing His scattered and despairing disciples together again. He was laying the foundation for His church.

A leadership function of equal importance is to *inform* and *explain.* This takes the most time of all and may even involve lengthy preparations. The Lord Jesus knew the Scriptures better than anyone else. He laid out for them everything in Scripture that shed light on the recent events, beginning with Genesis 3:15 and working His way forward to the prophecies in Isaiah about the suffering servant of the LORD, until He reached the messianic prophecies in the last books of the Old Testament. He freed those prophecies from Jewish presuppositions, and so the two men were able to see, with bright eyes, who the real messiah was, and shortly afterward to recognize Him standing before them!

To structure and regulate and order and summarize is another leadership activity to which we should turn our attention. The passage about the two men walking to Emmaus shows us the following structure: the Lord began with a summary which served as conclusion. "Was it not necessary for the Christ to suffer these things and to enter into His glory?" Then followed a systematic explication of this statement with reference to all sorts of relevant Scripture passages. Why did the Lord choose such a structure? Probably because of the shock effect of His statement that the Christ *had* to suffer these things. That, after all, was just what the disciples did *not* want to believe. They needed to be shocked if they were to listen properly to the material the Lord assembled by way of evidence, for they had to consider those passages in a *new* way.

In our conversations we usually follow a different method. First we gather the data or information, and then we draw a conclusion. But to sum things up and draw a conclusion as soon as possible gives a different structure to the conversation and is a good start for the next part of the conversation, or even for an entirely new conversation.

To give leadership also means that we motivate and stimulate and help and encourage others. The Lord's words made a tremendous impression on the two men walking to Emmaus. Their discouragement disappeared and was replaced by great joy. They were so full of the gospel that they could not wait until the next day to share their experiences with the other disciples — the very same evening they went back to Jerusalem! If you are to motivate people in a conversation, you must touch their heart, the source of the "springs of life" (Prov. 4:23).

When it comes to techniques to be used in conversation, we should also consider the element of personal confrontation that comes through in the value judgment Jesus uttered in His conversation with the men walking to Emmaus. That negative value judgment certainly did not leave the two men cold. A value judgment always strikes us in a personal way: we cannot respond to it as though we don't care what people say or think. Usually we cannot help either agreeing with it or contradicting

it. We may deny it by saying, "How in the world did you
reach *that* conclusion?" Or "How dare you say such a thing?"
Or "You haven't understood me at all. Your imagination is
running away with you!" Or we may quickly agree, as David
did when Nathan said to him, "You are the man!" David
responded, "I have sinned against the LORD" (II Sam. 12:13).
It was the same way with the two men walking to Emmaus.
Their heavy, unbelieving hearts had been touched and were
transformed into burning hearts, believing hearts.

Let's also pause for a moment to consider evaluation, the
time of reflection in which we ask ourselves whether the goal
was attained. Did we achieve what we hoped to in this conversation? If you have taken leadership in a conversation, it is
important to ask yourself this question. When the Lord Jesus
saw that the two men recognized Him as He broke bread with
them, He knew that the goal of the conversation had indeed
been attained: they recognized the Messiah, and they believed.
After the Lord disappeared, they talked excitedly about what
had happened: "Were not our hearts burning within us while
He was speaking to us on the road, while He was explaining
the Scriptures to us?" (Luke 24:32) They recognized that they
had been corrected and turned away from their unbelief.

Evaluation always keeps one eye fixed on the future. Was
the goal of the conversation reached, and are we thereby finished with the matter at hand? Or must there be some contin-
uation, whether in future conversations or in some action to be
taken? And if the goal was not reached, what then? Should we
repeat the conversation, perhaps adding some additional goals,
or should we simply accept the negative result? And can we
determine why the goal was not reached? Were we at fault in
sloppy preparation, or was our plan poorly executed? Should
we try it once again? These questions all point to the future.

And as long as we are busy with evaluation, we should also
focus on the non-material side of the conversation. What was
the atmosphere like? How did it influence the result? What
were the relations between the conversation partners in terms

of levels? Were there two equal partners, or was one subordinated to the other?

What is best of all is to conduct the evaluation together with one's conversation partner. Was it a good conversation? If office-bearers would dare to ask such questions at the end of a visit, they would show themselves to be both wise and courageous!

Chapter 13

Structuring the Conversation

Goals and phases

When two people "happen" to get involved in a discussion, they usually don't concern themselves about the *structure* of their conversation. And it makes sense for them not to do so, for if the conversation has no express purpose, it cannot have a specific goal either. The two discussion partners may be aware of a certain social pleasure that comes of talking together, which in turn gives some direction to the conversation: they will then look for pleasant things to talk about. When they have exhausted one subject, they will pick up another pleasant theme or perhaps tell some jokes. A conversation of this sort will wander around: its very lack of structure may be regarded by the discussion partners as contributing their enjoyment of it. Yet, because amazing things can happen in a conversation, such a discussion can suddenly change in character and end in a proposal of marriage, for example, or it may be used by one of the parties to make a joyful announcement.

Two or more people can also get together with the express intent of talking about a given subject or discussing a problem. Acts 11 takes us to Jerusalem, where the apostles and other believers were discussing the question what Peter was up to. Why did he go into the house of a pagan and eat with the uncircumcised? Surely that was wrong! In such a case the conversation can only have an outcome if it is carried on in an orderly way, that is, if it has a structure that enables the discussion partners to solve the problem or think their way out of it or beyond it. Anyone who has a fixed purpose will map out a route that enables him to reach his purpose. In the case of a conversation we divide the discussion into phases or stages which we will go through in order, if at all possible.

Our example from Acts 11 gives us a structure that is widely applicable. First we need the necessary and correct information. The troubled brothers had heard what happened in Caesarea, but they did not know about the events leading up to it. This gap was now filled in by Peter. With this accomplished, the issue of substance could be addressed. What were they to think of it?

When we consider this final question, we should pause and ask what criteria were being employed. Among the believers in Jerusalem, there was no disagreement that if God had indeed given the Holy Spirit to those pagans, that would settle the issue. Thus the discussion could quickly move into the third phase, namely, summarization, which included stating the conclusion that was reached. God, it appeared, had extended to those pagans the gift of conversion unto life. Thus what we have in this example is a structure composed of three phases: (i) gathering of adequate information, (ii) discussion, including an application of the information to the case at hand, and (iii) summarization and conclusion.

Now, it would be the death of genuine conversation if we stubbornly and high-handedly tried to impose such a structure on every conversation we conducted. When a man is furious or a woman is crying, with the result that the story is coming out in a disordered manner, in fits and starts, you cannot just say, "Get a grip on yourself: cool down, and wipe away those tears. And when you tell me what's going on, limit yourself to the information I really need." Still, this does not mean that you should not have some sort of structure in mind when you are taking the leadership in a conversation. You know that if you are to get anywhere, you must be properly informed. As you seek the information you need, bear in mind what I said earlier about the proper posture or attitude for conversation, and also about the spirit of love and sympathy that is needed.

I once heard a minister give the following advice (which probably will not strike you as terribly loving) about the first phase of an emotional conversation in which someone's "problem" is being laid out: "The first fifteen minutes, or perhaps half an hour, you should just whine along with the person you're talking to. But finally, you have to call a halt to it." Such a display of commiseration, abruptly broken off, might not seem genuine, and so I cannot recommend it. We must not play games with people. We have to work hard to create a sphere of trust, so that everything important eventually gets said. Usually you will not have to do all that much talking yourself. By being reflective you are showing that you understand the problem, or that you are touched by the sorrow or loss — but that's not the same as whining along! The reaction you get when you take such an approach will tell you whether you are on the right track.

After a period of time, which could be either long or short, the second phase of the conversation begins. If we have spent forty-five minutes or an hour sorting out our ideas, a decision about the further course of the conversation has to be made. At that point we should not expect to be able to round out the discussion and come to some resolution in another fifteen minutes or so. Even if we have plenty of time at our disposal, we still have to consider whether to continue the conversation; what we might do instead is make an appointment to talk further some other day. Such an intensive conversation demands a great deal of energy, and once the supply of energy is exhausted, there is a strong possibility that the conversation will come to an impasse, and that we will not be clever or creative enough to find a way out.

A decision of this sort is also needed in the course of an evangelistic conversation. We are sometimes so happy that we made it into the house and now have a chance to sit and talk that we squirm and fidget as we wait impatiently for our conversation partner to finish what he is saying, for we still have not had a chance to present the gospel! And if our presentation has to be squeezed into ten minutes or so, we will surely fall back on a pre-packaged speech or homily, which our conversation partner will probably find disappointing, for it has no connection with what was said before. The person we are visiting will then conclude: "What *I* said was probably not important. These people simply don't listen. I won't invite them into my house again." To avoid such a reception, it may be wise to break off the encounter after the first phase and set a time to get together again and talk further. The middle part of the conversation, in which we speak somewhat more directively, demands a substantial stretch of time.

Once we sense that we have won the trust of our conversation partner, there are the following possibilities. (i) *Confrontation.* It may be that our conversation partner has uttered contrary statements. Suppose it is a young lady who has been sexually abused by her father. She may say, "I won't put up with it any longer — I'm leaving the house!" But perhaps she also says, "I don't want to bring shame on my father, and I certainly don't want him to wind up in prison!" By bringing such statements together and comparing them, it becomes possible to see which course of action will eventually have to be taken.

(ii) *Appealing to norms.* Which norms are applicable to this situation? To what extent is our conversation partner aware of having to abide by certain norms? What about a person who has a son or daughter romantically involved with an unbeliever and who then refuses to regard that son or daughter as a member of the family any longer? Could it be that our conversation partner is aware that he or she is not living up to the relevant norms? Perhaps you are told, "I feel so guilty about the way I have treated my children!" But it may also be that the applicable norms are simply not accepted as valid and relevant to the situation. "Nowhere in the Bible does it say that you have to go to church twice on Sunday." Or, "If two people really love each other and have promised to be faithful to each other, there's nothing wrong with them living together."

Are we dealing with Christian norms, or with norms generally accepted in society at large?

(iii) *Helping, comforting, admonishing, encouraging.* Perhaps you should speak some careful words of comfort and salvation, preferably in question form. The question form does not mean that you are uncertain: you use it because you do not want to put words in the mouth of your conversation partners if they have already reached certain conclusions on their own. Suppose a woman has just been visited by her doctor and has received test results indicating the she has cancer. Not even surgery can help her. Her husband and her doctor are seated by her bed. It is quiet for a moment. Then she utters words that no human being can pronounce in his own strength: "Now, too, we have good reason to praise God."

Let us suppose that a minister is visiting a middle-aged man in the hospital who has just heard the same prognosis: he has cancer, and there is nothing the doctors can do about it. The man says, "Pastor, I do not understand why I am being punished so severely. I'm frightened of pain, and I have often prayed to the Lord to take me away in my sleep without pain or fear or a death struggle. O God, why? Why?" The pastor then asks him, "You said, 'O God, why?' Are you able to say, 'O *my* God, why?'"

Not much more was said in this second example. The sick man needed time for the struggle. Later there would have to be a third phase in his conversation with the pastor. But once the third phase is undertaken, some sort of resolution must be sought.

The first thing to be considered is whether you are the right person to offer the kind of assistance that is needed. Should someone else enter the picture at this point? Is professional help needed? If you are dealing with a person who is deeply depressed and you point to God's promises, you may well make the depression even worse, because his inability to accept those promises makes his sense of guilt still greater.

Moreover, if you are indeed the right one to deal with the

suffering person, it may still turn out that *one* conversation is not enough. Some follow-up conversations may be needed. And if you are able to bring the conversation to some resolution, you must review the nature of the conversation in your own mind, for this information will be important for the direction taken as the the conversation is concluded.

Conversations cannot be summed up under a single descriptive label; yet there are usually some central themes that can be pointed out. As types we could identify: the *informative* conversation, the *news-only* conversation, the *problem-oriented* conversation, the conversation geared to *comfort,* the conversation aimed at *admonition,* and the conversation in which *advice* is offered.

If you are conducting an *informative* conversation because your conversation partner was unaware of certain matters or did not know about certain customs or missed out on some lessons or has difficulty understanding some concepts, then you yourself will probably do most of the talking. Yet you will wonder whether everything you passed on has been properly understood and retained. At the end of the conversation you will try to get the other person to talk, for only then will it become apparent whether the conversation was genuinely informative and instructive.

This is not the way you would proceed in a *news-only* conversation. You might begin such a conversation by passing on some bad news. For example, you might say, "You asked to make public profession of your faith, but the church council has decided not to allow this because it does not see the proper motives operative behind your request."

In the second phase of such a conversation, the following reactions may be encountered. *Aggression:* "I can't accept that — I'll appeal to the classis. What in the world does that stupid church council think it's doing?" Or *regression:* "I was afraid, when I asked, that there would be a problem. Well then, I guess I won't make public profession after all." Or *denial:* "It appears to me that the church council has made a mistake. If you give them some more information, I'm sure they'll make the right decision about this matter when they meet again next week." Or *acceptance:* "Yes, you're right. I was tired of going to confession classes, and I really hadn't thought the matter through very carefully. I wasn't even aware that the church council would be concerned about my motives." Depending on the reaction we get in this second phase, we will have to move to some sort of resolution in the third phase.

In the case of a *problem-oriented* conversation, the problem first comes on the table. In the middle part of the conversation, we strive for some clarity as to what the problem is. Could it be that there is some other problem in the background behind the matter in the foreground on which we are focusing our attention? If we get somewhere in this second phase, we must be on our guard, as we enter the third phase, against the dangers of the "diagnosis and prescription" model. This label refers to the doctor who, after establishing a diagnosis for his ailing patient (who knows little about medical matters), gives him a prescription. In our conversation we are not generally in the position of an expert speaking to a conversation partner whom we can then treat as a mere layman. In other words, a "diagnosis and prescription" model doesn't fit here. When it comes to the third phase, a problem-oriented conversation should have clarified the problem in such a way that the solution (assuming that there is one) suddenly becomes apparent, and so our conversation partner has something to take away with him.

In a conversation in which *advice* is being passed on, we should also be careful not to fall into the "diagnosis and prescription" model by acting as though it is simple and straightforward for an expert to figure out what to do. In many cases the advice we give is taken so seriously by those who seek it that it simply becomes their decision. Such a situation can all too easily become an unhappy one.

An engaged couple go to a minister because the man has homosexual inclinations and has serious doubts as to whether he should get married. The minister advises, "Just go ahead and get married. The two of you will be able to overcome those homosexual inclinations if you pray for this together and if you do not encourage the homosexuality in any way but struggle against it." In time this woman and the children she bore are abandoned as her husband goes off to live with a homosexual friend. And she cannot understand how the minister could have given such advice, for they did pray about the matter, and she did take her husband back time and again and forgave him each time for leaving her. Yet, when the minister gave this positive advice, he himself was plagued by grave doubts, which were wrongly downplayed. His advice became their decision.

It would be much better to weigh all the pros and cons of such a situation and then say, "That's about as far as I can go in terms of helping you with your decision. Think it over and see whether you might not want to consult a specialized social worker. Consider the matter carefully. Pray to God for wisdom, and then come and tell me what decision you have come to, and on what grounds."

Praying and Bible reading

The minister said, "Pray to God for wisdom." Naturally, the question arises: why didn't the minister pray with the engaged couple himself? This would surely have been in order. But I didn't include this element in the scenario I sketched because I wanted to make a certain point. There are some Christians who believe that there must be praying and Bible reading if one of the conversation partners is an office-bearer, because prayer and Bible reading are what makes such an encounter a *pastoral conversation*! I want to take issue with this notion.

People can converse in truly Biblical fashion without ever opening the Bible. It could well be that such young people can lay their needs before the LORD more effectively than the minister can. Yet what I would plead for is that Bible reading and prayer in the course of such a visit become somewhat more customary and expected than is currently the case.

Nowadays we talk a lot about being *authentic.* This curious expression seems to mean that all that was once customary or traditional must somehow be regarded as inauthentic or less than genuinely meant — mere form or pretense. People fail to realize the great value of customs and do not understand the extent to which they give structure to our lives. Yet this is not to deny that when we act in accordance with our customs, we must do so in a self-conscious way so that they do not become mere repetition. There is nothing wrong with something being customary, provided it is meaningful and we are aware of its meaning.

There are some ministers and elders who, when visiting a mother who has just given birth, chat with her for a while and then disappear with a wave after about fifteen minutes. Others simply send a postcard. That certainly seems friendly enough, but it is contrary to the long-established pattern, and so it generally leads to disappointment, or even an aggressive response: "If he can't be bothered to come, he can just as well keep his postcard too!" Or, "I had expected that we would at least pray together." Now, I do not deny that circumstances sometimes make the visit difficult: there may be a crying baby in the room, or a nurse bustling about trying to get some work done. Yet a conscientious office-bearer will still ask for a few moments of silence so that he can read a passage of Scripture, say a few words about it, and pray with the mother he is visiting. If this is completely out of the question because of special circumstances, it is better to come back on another occasion. All of this need not be experienced by the mother as a formality if the Scripture passage is carefully chosen, that is, if the office-bearer places a Biblical message clearly before the sister he is visiting and then prays in heartfelt way.

When members of the congregation visit each other on a so-cial basis, or seek someone out because he is having difficulties or problems or has fallen ill or perhaps because of some good fortune that has come his way, they often do not get around to praying together or reading from the Bible. Why is this? When a woman seeks out another woman because she is alone and lonely, or because she is in spiritual need, or is seriously ill, or because of some other reason, she may wind up talking about all sorts of seemingly trivial matters (in a different way than a man, for men seem to have their own topics), but surely she will also talk about the blessings of salvation that are ours in Christ. Shouldn't she then also be bold enough to suggest that they pray together?

Chapter 14

Rejected Comfort

This chapter is about the difficulty of offering true comfort. All too often we wind up speaking in beautiful, completely developed sentences that have the effect of hiding our embarrassment and real feelings. Let me give you a couple of examples of well-meant comfort that winds up embittering people.

A mother with married children has ten grandchildren. In the family of her daughter and son-in-law, who themselves are not all that young anymore, a son was born six months ago. The baby's parents are crazy about him, and so is his grandmother. But one morning the baby is found dead in its crib! This is such a blow for the parents that that it seems they simply cannot be comforted. The grandmother is also deeply upset and disappointed. Every time she thinks about it, the tears flow. One day her minister comes to see her. He is well aware of the situation and knows the whole family. He uses quite a few words as he comforts her, for he sees that her grief is intense and deep. What he says is surely well intended; the loss of this child, after all, is a very serious matter. Yet he points out that the Lord has left this grandmother with nine other grandchildren she should also be thinking about. She still has a lot to be thankful for.

Later the grandmother reflects on this visit and says to herself, "If he has nothing better than that to say, he should stay away!" The minister's way of offering comfort *trivializes* the loss: when you have ten grandchildren, the loss of one of them is indeed a serious matter, but it is not quite so catastrophic as she made out. In effect her "comforter" was saying, "Your grief is too great in relation to what you have actually lost."

In such a situation the minister could have taken a different tack. He could have inquired into the cause of death and been told that it was an instance of crib death. He might then have said, "Crib death! We didn't hear much about that years ago, but once you run into a case or two, you discover that it happens more often than many people realize." In taking such an approach, the minister would be making the situation out to be somewhat less exceptional than the grandmother might have thought: actually, crib death is common enough that you should count yourself lucky if it bypasses your family.

Yet it is really of no comfort to be told that your child (or grandchild) has died in the same way as thousands of others. The minister is offering a *generalization.* It's really a terrible thing, when you think about, to toss someone's grief on a huge pile of human misery — the grief of people all suffering for the same sort of reason. If you receive this sort of comfort, you conclude that your grief is not being taken seriously.

If we stick with the same situation by way of example, we can ask what happens when we begin to *philosophize* or *theologize.* For example, we could talk about the *meaning* of suffering. If a person's life is dominated by suffering, he cannot help but ask: Why me? Why must *I* suffer all of this? What is God trying to teach me?

Was there something wrong in the lives of the parents of the child who died, and was God now punishing them? If so, why did *the child* have to die? There are many difficult questions of this sort that could be raised and discussed. We might seek answers for such questions, but we know in advance that we will not find them. We were busy talking with the people who are afflicted, but where was the comfort?

In our perplexity we could think of all sorts of things to say, perhaps drawing on *psychology.* We might offer a diagnosis like this one: You were unusually attached to this child. Could that be so because he was the son of your favorite daughter? Aren't you too much wrapped up with her in her sorrow? And isn't it the worst thing of all that *she* simply will not be comforted?

We could also take a somewhat sterner approach and declare that *action* is needed — something must be done. For
example: "If you continue this way, you'll only get more and
more upset. You sit here the whole day alone in the house —
you should get out! Why don't you call a travel agent and
make arrangements for a spring vacation in Europe? You need
some diversion; you need people around you; you need some
company."

You could also *offer advice*, which would be a bit less high-
handed: "Don't you think you are too preoccupied with this
death? Shouldn't you take some distance from it? Isn't there
a nice book around the house that you've been wanting to read
for a long time? Why don't you take a walk? I know you love
to walk! You can't make a career of dwelling on this death.
You have to start to think about yourself again."

There are still more ways of offering comfort in which we
seem concerned primarily with cutting a fine figure ourselves
and not being left without something to say. Such concerns
often seem to take precedence over our stated purpose of comforting the bereaved and showing them our love. Even such
a statement as "You shouldn't be so sad about this, for you
know that the baby is in heaven" can come across as lacking
in compassion.

Chapter 15

Before and After the Conversation

And when they arrest you and deliver you up, do not be anxious beforehand about what you are to say, but say whatever is given you in that hour; for it is not you who speak, but it is the Holy Spirit. Mark 13:11

Preparation

In discussing the preparations we make for a wholesome spiritual conversation, I draw your attention first to the text above. Yet I would not want you to conclude that this text suggests that no preparation is needed at all since the Spirit will somehow do the talking for us!

The text indicates very specifically in what situation we may expect the Spirit to give us words to speak. If we are arrested and brought before the judge, if we have to speak before kings and governors, often after spending considerable time in prison, *then* we may expect the help of God's Spirit as we give an account of ourselves. The Spirit will enable us to testify of Jesus Christ before all who turn against Him and persecute His children.

We find a beautiful example of this in Acts 25 and 26, where Paul speaks on his own behalf before King Agrippa and the procurator Festus. His concern was to proclaim the gospel before these rulers, who surely did not lead unblemished lives (Festus was open to bribes, and Bernice was both the wife and the sister of Agrippa!), in hopes of leading them to faith, and he did not spend much time arguing for his own innocence.

And not only Paul, but many martyrs — even slaves who did
not know how to read or write — have in times of persecution
testified to their unwavering faith as they stood before their
judges.

In a situation where believers face persecution and impris-
onment, proper preparation for an audience is usually all but
impossible. But if *we* are preparing for a meeting with someone
as we work on behalf of the church, we have every opportunity
to make a few notes, perhaps select a Bible passage to be read
aloud, and think of a few words to say about the passage. We
could look through a devotional booklet for some ideas, or we
could bring a poem.

If we know whom we will be visiting and what the subject
of our conversation will be, we will try to imagine the thoughts
and feelings of our conversation partner before we get there.
Then we can consider carefully the best way to begin the conversation, for a bad start is not easily corrected and overcome.
A conversation is never ours to make alone; we are always dependent for its success on our conversation partner. Therefore
we must be prepared to be flexible. Yet you can make plans in
advance about what to discuss — and how. Such preparation
is always meaningful. But if the encounter unfolds in a way
you did not expect, it is more important to have a good conversation anyway than to stick stubbornly to some plan you
made in advance, for if you are too inflexible, you will not be
in a position to listen. Then you will wind up delivering a
monologue rather than carrying on a dialogue.

Your preparation should also include prayer. You should
pray for yourself, that the Holy Spirit will illumine you, and
you should not forget to pray for the person you are going to
visit.

In addition to these specific preparations for a conversation,
there is also some general preparation you could undertake,
preparation that will help you in connection with any conversation. There are two dimensions you could work on: conver-

sational techniques and the subject matter of the conversation. As for the former, there are various aids available nowadays. For example, there are courses you could take in which you are assigned listening exercises. You are then trained in posing open questions. The conversations are recorded on tape and analyzed. This makes it possible for you to work systematically on the proper attitude or posture to assume for a conversation (see Chapter 6).

To prepare yourself in general for the subject-matter side of a conversation takes years. It requires knowing the Bible and the confessions of the church intimately, so that you can draw on them freely in conversation. You must also know something about church history, especially the errors of earlier centuries and the various sects and theological divisions of our own time. And there's still more! You should be abreast of current events, which requires knowing what people are reading about nowadays in the newspaper. You need to be aware why some people seem so aggressive, staging demonstrations, provoking the police, engaging in vandalism and violent attacks, committing murder, and undertaking guerilla warfare. You should also have some idea why so many people take refuge in a seeming indifference and apathy, why others live for enjoyment only and get drunk often, and why some commit suicide. What makes people tick today? What drives men and women? What — if anything — do they still trust?

Look again at the text above this chapter. Do not be concerned if you must give an account of yourself in a time of persecution before the judge or the authorities, for the Holy Spirit will speak for you.

In Acts 7 we read about Stephen, who was the first Christian martyr. There was an accusation against him: he was supposed to have spoken slanderous words against the temple and the law, declaring that Jesus of Nazareth would break down the temple and would change the customs which had been handed down by way of Moses. But now Stephen began to justify his claims. The Council and all the others who were present saw his face shining as though it were the face of an angel. Clearly the Holy Spirit had come to his aid in this time of trial and was speaking for and through him. But notice the *content* of what was said: the Holy Spirit drew on Stephen's knowledge of *Moses and the prophets*. This was knowledge Stephen had picked up over many years beginning with his childhood and youth, knowledge he had at his fingertips. He quoted from Genesis, Exodus, Deuteronomy, Joshua, Samuel, Kings, Chronicles, Isaiah, and Amos. He quoted Scripture extensively, and seemingly with great enjoyment.

I will not go into the content of Stephen's address. I simply point to this episode to show that it is a mistake to trust in the Holy Spirit without at the same time studying God's Word constantly. Such an approach will lead to great disappointments and leave the believer uncertain.

Follow-up work

When a conversation is finished, you should not neglect to review it critically. Was it a good conversation? Would your conversation partner agree that it went well? (Remember what I said about evaluation in Chapter 11.) In most cases you will not be entirely satisfied with how it went. And this is as it should be, for a critical review should spur you on to do some follow-up work.

Suppose you have had a conversation with a father and mother who had their first child baptized some time ago. To your amazement you are told that they had not wanted to break with the custom of having children baptized, even though their own view is that parents should not make such a choice for a child. Instead the child should make the choice on his own when he is mature and independent. Naturally, you immediately challenged this line of argument, but as you look back on the conversation, you are not satisfied with how it went. The mother and father had thought about the issue over quite a period of time. They came up with all sorts of considerations: they maintained that there was no baptism of infants in the early church, but that people were only baptized after making a profession of their faith. You did not know what to say about all their arguments, and so you went home dissatisfied with your part of the conversation.

What action should you take? Study! Perhaps you have some books around the house that can answer the questions you now face; in that case, no further research will be needed. Or you may have to turn to your minister for further resources. Is there a brochure or booklet you could hand to the couple you visited (after you have studied it yourself, of course)? If there is, you should make an appointment to discuss this matter with them further, when you will be better prepared to deal with their arguments.

If you build up your knowledge and insight in such a carefully directed way, you will have at your disposal a virtual arsenal of weapons to draw from over the years. Then you will be well equipped whenever you enter upon such a struggle.

As you can see from this example, follow-up work does not only involve yourself but also (in many cases) your conversation partner. This becomes even more apparent when we consider conversations whose intent is mainly instructional. I think here of members of the congregation who did not have any Christian education or instruction in the faith during their childhood and youth, with the result that they have little knowledge of the Bible and the confessions of the church. I also think of people with mental handicaps of one sort or another, who cannot learn by way of the usual catechism materials. Some may suppose that offering instruction in the faith to people like this is exclusively the responsibility of the office-bearers, but this is a mistake. Ideally speaking, the members of the congregation who have the gifts for teaching should be plugged into this role, regardless of whether they are currently office-bearers. To be successful in such instructionally oriented conversations, it is important to come with a plan in which you spell out what material is to be dealt with, and in what way.

Another good example of a follow-up visit is the visit you would make to someone who has just lost a loved one. When people are grieving, it is almost always necessary to visit them more than just once. This type of visit requires a great deal of sensitivity. It makes a difference whether you are dealing with a *man* who has just lost his marriage partner, or with a *woman* who has become a widow, or with *parents* who have lost a child in an accident. Remember that after the funeral the man returns to his work and the children go back to school, whereas the mother, staying home to manage the household, may suddenly find herself alone all day. People work through their grief differently if they have a job or a schoolroom to return to than if they are retired and have no work or regular activity to occupy them. An older person who has just become a widow or widower is in danger of falling into utter apathy, so that even the little bit of work that remains to be done, such as preparing warm meals for oneself, is neglected.

For ministers and other office-bearers, it is important to have a policy regarding how often one visits the bereaved. For example, one might decide to come two or three times during the first week after a death has taken place, twice during the second week, and only once in the third week. Such a commitment to visit should not be made on the condition that nothing else comes up unexpectedly in the congregation; it must be possible to make the promised visits even if there are more deaths and serious illnesses. That's why it is important not to promise too much. In an emotional situation one may quickly say, "You can count on it that we will visit you regularly — we won't forget you." This promise may be very well intended, but it would be better not to make such a commitment at all if we are not able to live up to it. And so it is important that some sort of visiting schedule be established, one that may well involve members of the congregation, so that we can be sure the visiting is not neglected.

As a final example, I turn to conversations with those who are alone, and perhaps lonely. They may be alone because their marriage partner has died. Or they may be the only one left of a pair or set of brothers and/or sisters who were living together in their later years. There is also a great deal of loneliness among younger people who live on their own. There are even lonely people living within families or multi-person households of one sort or another! Perhaps you cannot think of any people who fit into the latter category, but if you visit unmarried adults on a regular basis, you will be struck by the agonizing loneliness some of them endure.

If you make it your business to visit some lonely person regularly, you may not be done with it until he or she has died. I'm talking here about conversations that must repeatedly be undertaken anew because a sense of community is kindled through the conversation. Your visit makes it possible for such a person to break through the loneliness for a moment and to have a sense of belonging to a larger group.

It should be obvious that this work cannot all be shoved off onto the office-bearers. The deacons will of course be particularly busy in seeing to it that no one who suffers from sickness, loneliness or poverty lives without comfort and support in the church of Christ — that is their special responsibility. Therefore they will be active and will set a good example for all the members. By serving those who are in need, they will stimulate others to rise to the challenge, for work of this sort requires a great deal of time and energy. No one in the church should be (or remain) lonely.

Follow-up visits will sometimes lead to new discoveries. For example, you might discover that what you originally took to be a rather strong reaction to a specific disappointment is really something larger and more general — perhaps a case of serious depression. If a good relationship has been established through your visits, and if the suffering person has truly come to trust you, you must be sure to continue with such visits. Although you are not in a position to practice psychotherapy, you might well, at the appropriate moment, point to the availability of psychologists, psychiatrists and psychotherapists of various sorts who are able to help such people. If you do so, you are not thereby withdrawing from the case!

A man and woman who have been married for some years and would love to have children might approach their minister with the question whether childlessness is the path that God wants them to take in their marriage. Or are they permitted to make use of modern medical means that might make pregnancy possible? Such a question can be dealt with in one — or perhaps more — conversations. Obviously, if the minister and the married couple together come to the conclusion that some of the new possibilities may be used, intensive conversations with the family doctor and the specialist will follow. Here we have an example that illustrates the general rule to be followed in such helping conversations: we must ask ourselves whether *we* have the expertise to render the assistance that is requested. If not, we should refer our conversation partner to someone who does.

Reporting and confidentiality

Sometimes it is necessary to make notes on a conversation. Reliance on notes can help you avoid needless repetition in a subsequent conversation.

When a report is made on a conversation or a home visit, e.g. at a church council meeting, or in a discussion with a professional person who may get involved in the case, or at a staff meeting of some sort, the question of confidentiality comes up. In Chapter 6 I wrote about the importance of creating a sphere of discretion, trust and personal concern. When people place their trust in us and tell us about intimate aspects of their lives, we cannot be careful enough with their confidences. It is simply scandalous that some people betray such trust in order to advance their own interests. Almost as reprehensible is the practice of passing on a few juicy tidbits — after swearing one's hearers to secrecy, of course! — for the sake of entertainment, so that people will say, "You hear some interesting stories from that fellow."

The question becomes especially difficult when you ask yourself: of all that I have heard, what must I report at the meeting of the church council? As you try to assess what you should include and what you should leave out, ask yourself as you consider a given detail: would the brother or sister have told me this if he or she was well aware that I must give the church council a substantive report on this visit? Elders and deacons also have their professional confidences which they may not divulge.

Reporting on people's problems, whether at a church council, a staff meeting, or some other setting, must always be done in a sober and discreet spirit. If you are seeking advice on a certain problem you have run into, you are generally better off not asking colleagues about it. The one wants to know more about this aspect, and the other pursues something else that interests him in particular. The result is that various details become "public," details that cause considerable pain and shame for the church member from whose life they are drawn. It is much better to get *permission* from the brother or sister first and then take the problem to the minister or an especially wise or experienced colleague or fellow office-bearer. If you have once betrayed the trust people have placed in you, you will find that others whom you visit as you go about your work do not want to open up to you.

Chapter 16

Carry on a Holy Conversation

Now may our Lord Jesus Christ Himself and God our Father, who has loved us and given us eternal comfort and good hope by grace, comfort and strengthen your hearts in every good work and word.   II Thess. 2:16–17

In Lord's Day 33 of the Heidelberg Catechism we find a discussion of the true conversion of man, which includes the dying away of the old man and the rising up of the new man. If we lay particular emphasis on the notion that the old man must *more and more* die away and then be renewed, it becomes obvious that true conversion is a *process.* It is not something with which we are done in just a moment; rather, it is a continuing task. Hence Paul says to Timothy: "Discipline yourself for the purpose of godliness" (I Tim. 4:7).

True conversion includes the doing of good works. When we talk about good works, we usually think in terms of good *deeds.* But Lord's Day 45 of the Catechism indicates that *prayer* is the most important "good work," and the text I quoted at the beginning of the chapter speaks of "every good work and *word."* Holy conversation counts as part of "every good work and word," for it involves talking in a believing way that honors God.

We should realize that the dying away of the old man, more and more, as the Catechism says, also has a bearing on the conversations we conduct, for in this area of our lives we also have to fight against the sinful element within us. But we have

102

the hope of being able to speak in a way that is in harmony with the will of God. This should give us comfort whenever we see that a given conversation has gone wrong through some fault of our own. It can also encourage us if we are inclined to believe that we are not capable of carrying on a holy conversation. If we try hard, we will fall down and rise up again many times, and in the process we will discover that we are, after all, able to carry on a holy conversation. We can make genuine progress, and after a while we may see steady improvement in the way we conduct our spiritual conversations. The most beautiful thing of all is when your conversation partner says (even though you yourself were not quite satisfied with the way it went), "That was a fine conversation!"

Sometimes we wrongly conclude that we are not able to do something we have been asked to do, even though we have already managed something like it successfully in the past. In such a case we fail to see the connection between what we have done before and what we now say we cannot do. Some mothers, for example, speak boldly and openly with their children about the LORD — who He is and how children must ask, in all matters great and small, "What does God want of us, and how do we know what He wants?" But those same mothers may dread visiting the sick or calling on a Christian neighbor lady to talk with her about the dreadful television programs she watches. If we have learned how to speak about salvation with our own children, then surely we are not undertaking anything new or different when we speak with other adults about it.

Young men may seek each other out to discuss problems in their lives. When they do so in faith, they are conducting holy, spiritual conversations. But some of them, when they are elected elders or deacons in later years, think they should decline to serve because they are incapable of conducting pastoral conversations. They forget that they were already involved in holy conversations when they were young men!

This little book is intended to be of assistance to both new and experienced office-bearers, and also other church members, including men and women, young and old. It is for every member who wishes to qualify himself through practice to speak even more boldly and joyfully about the salvation that is ours in Christ. "Let us hold fast the confession of our hope without wavering, for He who promised is faithful; and let us consider how to stimulate one another to love and good deeds" (Heb. 10:23–24).